Dockside Reading

Dockside Reading

DUKE UNIVERSITY PRESS
Durham and London   2022

Hydrocolonialism
and the Custom House
Isabel Hofmeyr

© 2022 Duke University Press. All rights reserved
Project editor: Lydia Rose Rappoport-Hankins
Text designed by Courtney Leigh Richardson
Cover designed by A. Mattson Gallagher
Typeset in Portrait Text and Helvetica Neue by Copperline Book Services

Library of Congress Cataloging-in-Publication Data
Names: Hofmeyr, Isabel, author.
Title: Dockside reading : hydrocolonialism and the custom house / Isabel Hofmeyr.
Description: Durham : Duke University Press, 2022. | Includes bibliographical references and index.
Identifiers: LCCN 2021016435 (print)
LCCN 2021016436 (ebook)
ISBN 9781478015123 (hardcover)
ISBN 9781478017745 (paperback)
ISBN 9781478022367 (ebook)
Subjects: LCSH: Customs inspection—Great Britain—Colonies. | Customhouses—Great Britain—Colonies. | Books and reading—Great Britain—Colonies. | Censorship—Great Britain—Colonies. | Copyright—Great Britain—Colonies. | Marks of origin—Social aspects. | Postcolonialism. | Great Britain—Colonies—Africa—Administration. | Cape of Good Hope (South Africa)—Politics and government—1872-1910. | Cape of Good Hope (South Africa)—Politics and government—1910-1994. | BISAC: LITERARY CRITICISM / Semiotics & Theory | HISTORY / Africa / South / Republic of South Africa
Classification: LCC HJ6891 .H64 2022 (print) | LCC HJ6891 (ebook) | DDC 382/.70941—dc23
LC record available at https://lccn.loc.gov/2021016435
LC ebook record available at https://lccn.loc.gov/2021016436

Cover art: Photograph of Durban harbor, 1870s. Courtesy of the Photographic Collection on Durban, Local History Museums' Collection, Durban.

Duke University Press gratefully acknowledges the Abraham and Rebecca Stein Faculty Publication Fund of New York University, Department of English, which provided funds toward the production of this book.

For Merle Govind

And in memory of
Bhekizizwe Peterson (1961–2021)

Contents

ix   Acknowledgments

1   Introduction. **Hydrocolonialism:** The View from the Dockside

27   1   **The Custom House and Hydrocolonial Governance**

39   2   **Customs and Objects on a Hydrocolonial Frontier**

49   3   **Copyright on a Hydrocolonial Frontier**

63   4   **Censorship on a Hydrocolonial Frontier**

77   Conclusion. **Dockside Genres and Postcolonial Literature**

85   Notes
103   Bibliography
117   Index

Acknowledgments

Like most books, this one took much longer than expected. It was started in Johannesburg, completed in New York, and, as the pandemic lockdown took hold, revised back in Johannesburg. Across these (and other) cities, many communities and networks have buoyed me and the project along.

The Department of African Literature at the University of the Witwatersrand (Wits) has been my intellectual home since 1984, and I have learned much from colleagues there across the years. The current incumbents—Grace Musila, Danai Mupotsa, and Khwezi Mkhize—have been comradely colleagues and interlocutors. As ever, Merle Govind has kept us all on track.

The Wits Institute for Social and Economic Research (WiSER) has been another welcoming space with generous colleagues: thanks to Keith Breckenridge, Adila Deshmukh, Najibha Deshmukh, Pamila Gupta, Shireen Hassim, Jonathan Klaaren, Phumeza "MJ" Majola, Achille Mbembe, Nolwazi Mkhwanazi, Hlonipha Mokoena, Sizwe Mpofu-Walsh, Tinashe Mushakavanhu, Richard Rottenburg, and Makhosazana Xaba. Special thanks to Sarah Nuttall for her leadership of WiSER, her intellectual stylishness, and her warm friendship. At WiSER I codirect a project, Oceanic Humanities for the Global South, with Charne Lavery, a colleague and friend extraordinaire whose intellectual verve has enriched both the project and this book. I have learned much from the graduate students and postdoctoral fellows on the project: Rabia Abba Omar, Anézia Asse, Jono Cane, Confidence Joseph, Meghan Judge, Jacky Kosgei, Luck Makuyana, Mapule Mohulatsi, Zoe Neocosmos, Ryan Poinasamy, and Oupa Sibeko.

In the Faculty of Humanities at Wits, several colleagues, present and past, have contributed to the making of this book: Joni Brenner, Dilip Menon,

Brenda Mhlambi, Dan Ojwang, Vish Satgar, Sue van Zyl, Michelle Williams, and Justine Wintjes. I am indebted to Michael Titlestad for his deep knowledge of all matters maritime. Colleagues further afield have assisted in various ways. Goolam Vahed, with characteristic generosity, provided information and references. Working on Africa and the Indian Ocean world has linked me to a merry band of scholars whose insights and conversation have flowed into this book: thanks to Sunil Amrith, Gabeba Baderoon, Rimli Bhattacharya, Antoinette Burton, Mwelela Cele, Sharad Chari, Stephen Clingman, Pradip Datta, Uma Dhupelia-Mesthrie, Jatin Dua, Sarah Duff, Mark Ravinder Frost, Betty Devarakshanam Govinden, Patricia Hayes, Saarah Jappie, Stephanie Jones, Preben Kaarsholm, Chris Lee, Pedro Machado, Johan Mathew, Phindi Mnyaka, Joyce Nyairo, Michael Pearson, Meg Samuelson, Margaret Schotte, Stephen Sparks, Tina Steiner, Julie Stephens, Lindy Stiebel, Lakshmi Subramanian, and Nigel Worden.

Over the past decade, I have taught biennially in the English department at New York University. This opportunity to parachute into the US academy has enriched this book considerably. Thanks to Raji Sunder Rajan, Una Chaudhuri, and Chris Cannon for setting everything up, and to Patty Okoh-Esene and Alyssa Leal for making each landing so smooth. In New York, Yvette Christiansë and Roz Morris are friends and hosts without peer. Lisa Gitelman, Andy Parker, and Meredith McGill know the best places in New York City, almost as many as Graeme Reid. The New York University English department is a collegial environment with wonderful scholars from whom I have learned a great deal: thanks to Pat Crain, Wendy Lee, Paula McDowell, Liz McHenry, Maureen McLane, Sonya Posmentier, Catherine Robson, Sukhdev Sandhu, Greg Vargo, Jini Kim Watson, and Robert Young, as well as colleagues from the Department of Comparative Literature, Mark Sanders and Emily Apter. Tanya Agathocleous, Ashley Cohen, Steph Newell, Leah Price, Stéphane Robolin, Gauri Viswanathan, and Kerry Bystrom provided diversions, ideas, and insights, as did Linda Gordon, Arvind Rajagopal, Anu Rao, Dina Siddiqi, and David Ludden. Nienke Boer and Nick Matlin advised me on coffee, as did Polly Park Hyman on galleries (and, back in Johannesburg, Merry Park on gardening). In Ann Arbor, David Cohen and the much-missed Gretchen Elsner-Sommer always took me to the paper shop; Madhumita Lahiri and S. E. Kile provided friendship, conversation, and spectacular Thanksgivings; and Derek Peterson is always an excellent colleague.

Parts of this book were presented at a range of seminars and talks. Thanks to the inviters: Saugata Bhaduri, Laura Doyle, Daniel Elam, Dishon Kweya, Alan

Galey, Debjani Ganguly, Isabel Karremann, Susann Liebich, Simi Malhotra, Dan Yon, and others already mentioned.

Back in Johannesburg, especially during lockdown, many networks, across many mediums, sustained me and this project. The writing group heard more about Customs and Excise than they had reckoned for: thanks to Cathi Albertyn, Elsje Bonthuys, Barbara Buntman, Catherine Burns, Sarah Charlton, Natasha Erlank, Nafisa Essop Sheik, Liz Gunner, Caroline Jeannerat, Srila Roy, Alison Todes, and the ever-mourned Tessa Hochfeld. My bridge companions—Jackie Cock, Sharon Fonn, Caroline Southey, Aubrey Blecher, Veronica Klipp, Dom Erlank, and Ingrid Obery—Zoomed me through lockdown. Clare Loveday's weekly wit and musical selections were a tonic. Reshma Bhoola got me walking, along with Helena Barnard (and the occasional sighting of Brendon Wolff-Piggott).

I was entertained by Bronwyn and the Quaranteens, the Cat Stories group, and the ever-witty Bookies. Thanks to Bronwyn Findlay; Kathryn Wheeler, cat sitter extraordinaire; Helen Becker and Michael Harmey; and Didi Moyle. Thanks also to Moggie Lewis and Solomon Manyathela. Ruth Becker, Helen Struthers, and Estelle Trengove jollied me along, as did Diana Charlton and Catherine Stewart. Elise and Kevin Tait and Jan and Angela Hofmeyr and their lineages in Cape Town, Johannesburg, and London offered ongoing and unstinting support.

In Cape Town, Carolyn Hamilton, Pippa Skotnes, Sandy Prosalendis, and John and Alice Parkington provided prelockdown hospitality and collegiality. In the days when we could still travel, Annie Coombes, Deborah James, Patrick Pearson, Wayne Dooling, and Ruth Watson afforded friendship and hospitality for the traveler in London and Oxford.

Thanks to the marvelous professionals as Duke University Press, especially Courtney Berger for her intellectual imagination and foresight. The readers of the manuscript offered astute and generous comment, especially the patient reader 2.

This book is dedicated to my beloved colleagues Merle Govind and Bhekizizwe Peterson with whom I worked for many decades. Their integrity, generosity, wisdom, and humor continue to be an inspiration.

On June 15, 2021, Bheki left us. Our loss is immeasurable but, as Gabeba Baderoon said in her tribute to him, he is our "forever" person. His towering intellectual legacies have, and will continue to guide generations of students and scholars.

SECTIONS FROM THE INTRODUCTION, chapter 1, and chapter 3 were previously published in an earlier form in the following: "Colonial Copyright, Customs, and Indigenous Textualities: Literary Authority and Textual Citizenship," in *Indigenous Textual Cultures: Reading and Writing in the Age of Global Empire*, ed. Tony Ballantyne, Lachy Paterson, and Angela Wanhalla (Durham, NC: Duke University Press, 2020), 245–62; "Colonial Copyright and Port Cities: Material Histories and Intellectual Property," *Comparative Literature* 70, no. 3 (2018): 264–77; "Imperialism above and below the Water Line: Making Space Up (and Down) in a Colonial Port City," *Interventions* 22, no. 8 (2020): 1032–44, https://doi.org/10.1080/1369801X.2019.1659172; "In the Custom House," in *Further Reading*, ed. Matthew Rubery and Leah Price (Oxford: Oxford University Press, 2020), https://doi.org/10.1093/oxfordhb/9780198809791.013.3; and Isabel Hofmeyr, "Provisional Notes on Hydrocolonialism," *English Language Notes* 57, no. 1 (2019): 11–20. The National Research Foundation (South Africa) funded aspects of the research for this book.

Introduction

Hydrocolonialism
The View from the Dockside

In the early 1950s, the South African Customs and Excise Department issued a list of "Prohibited and Restricted Imports and Exports."[1] At first glance, the items listed are predictable: protected flora and fauna, historical relics, poisons, pests, perishables, dangerous chemicals, drugs, adulterated foods—all those items that needed to be kept in, or out, to ensure the safety, security, and identity of the nation and its citizens.

Yet tucked into the list are some surprises. On the *C* list, lurking among cacti, carcasses, crocodiles, curios, and cuttlefish, we encounter copyright. On the *T* list, ticks, toads, tomatoes, tortoises, and toy pistols lead us to trademark, positioned just above treacle. Other surprises are books (placed among bodies [dead], bones, and boots), printed matter (surrounded by prickly pears, primates [other than man], projectiles, and prunes), and censors (located between cement and centipedes).

These *T*s and *C*s did not mean that copyright, trademark, and censors were prohibited. Quite the opposite, in fact, since Customs and Excise used these mechanisms to exclude material deemed undesirable or counterfeit. In a colonial context, much printed matter came from outside the colony and was funneled through the port, where Customs inspectors checked to see that it was not pirated, seditious, obscene, or (in some regions) blasphemous. In the realm of Customs and Excise, copyright and censorship hence cohabit with a band of troublesome objects that putrefy, perish, catalyze, deceive, poison, and adulterate. No longer just an abstract legal form, copyright subsists alongside the ooze and treacle of organic matter. Censorship likewise acquires strange bedfellows: cement, crocodiles, and centipedes.

Considered from the viewpoint of Customs and Excise, copyright and censorship appear almost visceral, a quality seldom associated with intellectual property mechanisms generally imagined as noiseless and odorless. We think of copyright as a quiet and dry institution, moving through registry offices with the barely audible rustle of paper. In a similar vein, censorship is generally imagined as silently sinister, with anonymous bureaucrats burrowing away in Soviet-style buildings.

Yet in the colonial port, copyright policy and censorship protocols took shape in the clamor of the waterfront and its imbroglio of incoming cargo. These commodities might be diseased, contaminated, undesirable, illegal, or counterfeit. The hold of a vessel hummed with microbes, weevily maize, rotting cargo, dogs, parrots, reptiles, and cattle (both dead and alive). Ships burped bilgewater, extruded diseased human bodies, deposited animal carcasses, secreted seditious pamphlets and obscene objects, and disgorged "undesirable aliens."

Dockside Reading locates itself in this noisome location, tracking printed matter as it made its way from ship to shore and through the regulatory regimes of the Custom House. Like any border crossing, these transitions had logistic and economic implications. The maritime setting with its epidemiological and ecological dangers further complicated these processes in a way that land-based borders did not necessarily. Books were cargo to be moved, objects to be classified and taxed, and items to be checked for potential danger, whether ideological or epidemiological. These protocols were to have far-reaching implications for how colonial print culture and its associated institutions came to be defined.

This book is particularly concerned with two such institutions—copyright and censorship. Rather than an institution associated with authorship, copyright became conflated with cargo and commodity markings, specifically an inscription called the *mark of origin* ("made in England," "made in Australia," etc.), from the 1880s mandatory across the British Empire. In the case of British copyright, the imprint indicated that the book had been manufactured in Britain and was implicitly "white." Colonial copyright hence became a type of logistic inscription and racial trademark. With regard to censorship of printed matter, this material was not read so much as treated like other forms of cargo, its outside scanned for metadata markings (title, cover, publisher, place of publication, copyright inscription, language, script), its inside sampled for traces of offensive material. Books were "read" whole, as objects rather than texts.

Damp and humid, the dockside may appear an odd choice of site for analyzing books and print culture. Yet this setting proves surprisingly productive for tracing historical themes of print culture while also allowing us to address contemporary debates on reading. From Nathaniel Hawthorne onward, the Custom House has been thought of as an antiliterary space of cloddish bureaucrats. *Dockside Reading* offers a different perspective, arguing that the object-oriented reading of the wharfside, and the coastal environment in which it unfolded, provides examples of reading that are of considerable interest to a posthumanist, Anthropocene age.

The setting is southern Africa, with glances toward Australia and Jamaica and some passing mentions of India and Canada. The time is the late nineteenth and early twentieth centuries, although at times the narrative moves further back and forward. While centered on southern Africa, the book aims to give some sense of Customs as an institution in the British Empire and its role in revenue generation, state formation, and, somewhat unexpectedly, the shaping of colonial literary institutions. As chapter 1 explains in more detail, Custom Houses across the empire reported not to the Colonial or Foreign Office (or their predecessors) but to the Board of Customs. These reporting lines made Customs something of an empire within an empire, a situation that changed with the end of the navigation laws in the mid-nineteenth century, after which most Customs services fell under the colonial legislatures.

The terms *dockside reading* and *hydrocolonialism* constitute the larger framework for contextualizing these reading and hermeneutical protocols. The first term provides a microview of dockside procedures in relation to cargo and the way these were transferred to books. The second term furnishes a larger framework for theorizing these types of shore-shaped literary formations. I discuss each of these concepts in turn before setting out a chapter synopsis.

Dockside Reading

Port cities aim to pave the ocean and assert sovereignty over the conjuncture of land and sea. Yet they are unstable spaces, perched on reclaimed land and propped up by submarine engineering. On this artificial ground, port authorities have long designed regulatory media and regimes of identification to manage the coastal seam on which they work and to control the passage of people and cargo from ship to shore. Fashioned as much around commodities as human bodies, these regimens rely on object-oriented hermeneutical practices. I describe these protocols as *dockside reading*, shaped in the regulatory regimes and coastal environments of the colonial port city. I explore this topic in four stages: objects, bodies, books, and reading (the latter topic explored through Hawthorne's *The Scarlet Letter* with its famous Custom House).

Objects

Objects are the true protagonists of the port city, its raison d'être, shaping much of its infrastructure and architecture. Or, as a handbook on cargo observes, "A port is a shore-based installation for the transfer of goods from and to ships."[2] Such conveyance from ship to shore and through the port precinct is easier said than done. As Joseph Conrad observed, a discharged cargo, once spread across the quayside, seemed much larger and more disordered than it had in the hold from which it had emanated. This sprawl had to be lugged, heaved, classified, taxed, and transported. Conrad himself despised ports and their bureaucratic protocols. When a sailing ship docked, the "craft and mystery of the sea" withered before the "men of the earth." Driven by motives of "quick despatch and profitable freight," these "shore people" with their "lubberliness" tyrannized the ship and its crew.[3]

The shore people held views directly inverse to Conrad's. For them, a ship was generally an ark of "nuisances," a term from sanitary inspection much beloved of port authorities. Always a potential vector of disease, vessels discharged smelly stowage passengers and cargo, all still reeking of the ship. In some instances, both people and objects had to be fumigated before they could be admitted, or "landed," to use the language of the port itself. The term *landed* carries a dual meaning: the first is physical (being put on shore), the second legal, denoting legitimate entry, as in the phrase *landed immigrant*, someone lawfully and permanently admitted. The word was heavily inscribed in port protocol: the landing account, landing certificate, landing book, landing order, and, in Customs job descriptions, landing surveyor and landing waiter.[4] The prevalence of the term suggests that cargo had to be redeemed from the seafaring world (*unshipped*, to use another term) and inducted into the domain of shore people, as though the goods were undergoing an ecological rite of passage in moving from water to land, from one element to another.

In a colonial port, this passage was a perilous affair. In smaller ports and in the early history of larger ones, rickety port buildings and infrastructure perched precariously on sand spits where they were flooded by tidal rivers and battered by storms. Landing could involve dangerous journeys by lighter from the roadstead to a beach. In Durban cargo and passengers were carried by African laborers or ferried through the surf by Indian boatmen. For both people and objects, becoming landed was indeed a redemption from the ocean, a translation from one element to another.

Once they were on dry land, further rites awaited. These were precipitated by the colonial maritime boundary and its multiple routines of identification: epidemiological, fiscal, logistic, and legal. Cargo was scrutinized for signs of infection; it was classified for duty purposes; the markings on its exoskeleton were cross-checked with its accompanying documents; its contents were inspected to verify that they were not undesirable or diseased. These regimens made up the process of landing commodities, declaring them safe, legal, and productive, rendering up duty to the colonial fiscus.

This logistic work of the port was enabled by a dense semiotic environment of signs and symbols. Flares, buoys, beacons, and bells aimed to safeguard ships against the inconstant weather of the littoral. The port precinct itself was a semiotic mangle of cargo markings, semaphores, sirens, flags, signals, and documents. In about 90 percent of cases, cargo passed smoothly through this logistic relay without ever being opened, the consignments having been "read" by their exterior markings and associated documentation. In the remaining 10 percent of cases where goods fell under suspicion, a "stop note" was issued, and the cargo was opened, its contents searched, sniffed, tasted, counted, weighed, and measured. Such cases precipitated friction in the logistic chain, causing problems as much by the interruption they occasioned as by the contamination they portended.

Introduction 5

The hermeneutical practices of the dockside were shaped by an intimate interaction with objects and their accompanying logistic grammars.[5] Customs examiners grappled with these objects, arguing endlessly with each other and merchants about how they should be defined. Was a substance butter or margarine? Could medicinal herbs be the same as tea? Was a soup square the same as stock?[6] The Customs archive is filled with such debates, containing objects themselves (swatches of fabric, tinned condensed milk labels, packets of seeds) as well as endless correspondence on what exactly these things were.[7] Customs officials functioned as a species of dockside ontologist, decreeing what an object actually was, although they more than anyone else were aware of the contingency of such descriptions.

Customs classifications could not be unilaterally imposed on commodities. The nature and characteristics of each item decreed how it was to be examined, what kind of attention had to be paid to it, and where this would happen—in effect determining the work routines of Customs officials. Liquid required gauging; tea, sniffing; fabric, having its thread count reckoned. Heavy substances like iron or building stone had to be examined on the wharf, lighter, more portable material in warehouses.[8] The characteristics of objects determined where and how they could be marked: dried sheep- and goatskin, for example, resisted being stamped.[9] Objects exerted an influence on the built environment of the port. Meat required refrigerated storage; timber demanded cranes; wine in casks needed a temperature-regulated environment.[10] In larger ports, careers in the Customs and Excise service could be determined by particular commodities, with officials specializing in wood, tobacco, linen, or wine.[11]

Objects also influenced dockside protocols through the tariff schedules, manuals, compendiums, and inventories that shaped themselves around the things they enumerated. Like regulations on where and how objects were to be marked, or secret telegraph codes dedicated to particular commodities like cotton, the characteristics of the object determined how it would be cataloged. The cotton codes, for example, took account of color, quality, presence or absence of leaves and sand, stains, compression, and so on.[12]

These inventories and taxonomies have long fascinated scholars, famously provoking Michel Foucault's uneasy laughter in response to the list of animals in Jorge Luis Borges's imagined "Chinese Encyclopedia," which "shattered all the familiar landmarks of [Foucault's] thought" and implicitly defamiliarized the categories of Western rationality.[13] Yet paging through a tariff handbook is not unlike the Chinese encyclopedia in its strangeness. Take, for instance, the category "Boxes," from a South African tariff schedule of the 1920s, which includes the following:

Accumulator
Collar, leather
Drain, for tram rails
Fixture, wooden covered with coloured cloth
Jewellery, not cardboard
Mitre
Partitioned, for delivery of eggs
Partitioned, other
Cardboard printed
And cartons, cardboard
Dummy chocolate boxes
Wax cartons (jars) for food products.[14]

Rather than just being discursive grids, such lists illustrate how objects determine their own enumeration. Useful in this respect are Ian Bogost's observations on lists (or *ontographs*, as he calls them). For him, these are less discursive regimes than a form that captures the aloofness of objects. Lists approximate "the jarring staccato of real being" and decenter the "flowing legato" of supposed coherence. They "disrupt being . . . [and,] in doing so, a tiny part of the expanding universe is revealed through cataloging."[15]

Bogost belongs to what we might call the radical wing of object theorists, for whom there can be no pattern, context, or network with which to make comforting sense of an entity: all such schemas constitute a mere ontotheology. Graham Harman is unequivocal: "The network into which any object is thrust can only scratch the surface of its actuality"; it is "forever withdrawn from the swirl of exterior factors into which it is embedded."[16] Speculative realists like Steven Shaviro have softened this stance by outlining the legitimacy of both a radical object-oriented ontology approach and a network-oriented understanding. The former "addresses our sense of the thingness of things: their solidity, their uniqueness, and their thereness. . . . Every object is something, in and of itself, and . . . an object is not reducible to its parts, or to its relations with other things, or to the sum of the ways in which other entities apprehend it." A networked understanding, by contrast, is "an equally valid intuition: our sense that we are not alone in the world, that things matter to us and to one another, that life is filled with encounters and adventures."[17] This book veers toward the latter position, taking its cue from Jane Bennett, who has taught us about the "force of things" while demonstrating that networks and systems cannot be discounted: objects are "swirls of matter, energy and incipience that hold themselves together long enough to vie with the strivings of other objects, including the indeterminate momentum of the throbbing whole."[18]

Yet, whatever approach one takes, this book points to the Custom House as a rich site for thinking with and about objects. Indeed, the files in the Customs archives with their profusion of objects resemble an object-oriented ontology laboratory, while Harman sounds rather like a Customs officer debating the status of an object. The following sentence from Harman could as well be a description of a scene at the Custom House: "We never manage to rise above the massive clamor of entities, but can only burrow around within it. . . . The sanctuary of the human . . . has been jettisoned in favor of a dense and viscous universe stuffed absolutely full with entities."[19]

Taking a view from the colonial port widens debates on object ontologies that have thus far been focused on the Global North, seldom speaking to postcolonial contexts. In addition, as Katherine Behar points out, this scholarship has had little to say about those people who have been objectified.[20] A dockside vantage point gives us a longer trajectory on the histories of colonial object formation, which was wrought against a background of confusion between person and thing.

Bodies

Ports were shaped by their cargoes. Yet the historiographies of colonial port cities have had little to say on this theme, their attention focused on human bodies, especially those persons excluded by late nineteenth-century immigration-restriction policies that sought to enforce the global color line. As much distinguished scholarship has shown, these exclusionary practices shaped colonial forms of governance and the racialized categories of persons they elaborated.[21] The dramatis personae in these accounts have been immigration-restriction officials and the incoming passengers they dealt with. This book inserts Customs examiners and their objects more centrally into this picture, arguing that the dockside governance of objects had implications for bodies as well as books. Simply put, techniques for identifying and handling cargo were transferred to people.

This theme has been taken up by scholars of public health. Before the bacteriological revolution, objects were identified as sources of infection as much as, if not more than, humans were. Policies of fumigation, disinfection, and quarantine were first applied to objects, then to people.[22] On Ellis Island, immigrants were tagged, chalked, and marked as if they were cargo. Indentured Chinese laborers were classified as bonded merchandise.[23] This custodial orientation of Customs is especially apparent in its carceral language: commodities were routinely seized, detained, arrested, placed in custody or under observation, condemned, defaced, disposed of, or mutilated. In some cases, items could be corrected: an offending cover could be removed, an infected hide fumigated, an obscene image scraped from a "novelty pencil sharpener" or "keyhole tumbler" (but only by white labor).[24] Irredeemable objects were condemned and then "sentenced" to burning, drowning, or shredding into little pieces (as happened with some banned books).

The transfer of this carceral orientation to human bodies is clearest in the case of the Atlantic slave trade. Stefano Harney and Fred Moten argue that the enslaved constitute the first instance of "the shipped," branded like wine barrels and crammed into holds. For these two scholars, the Atlantic trade has to be understood in the framework of logistics (or what they call "logisticality"), a process in which the Custom House was centrally implicated.[25] Across the Atlantic world, Customs officials were intimately involved with receiving and processing enslaved people who were dutiable commodities. In southern Africa, the roots of Customs rest in Dutch and then British rule at the Cape. Like their Customs counterparts elsewhere in the empire, these officials worked in ports whose purpose and architecture had been shaped by the carceral prerogatives of receiving unfree labor, whether slaves, transported prisoners, or indentured workers. In many cases, the physical fabric of the port city itself had been built by this unfree labor. The objective of a colonial state based on a slave mode of production was to take in Black and brown bodies rather than exclude them. By contrast, immigration restriction aimed to keep such bodies out. While arcs of continuity certainly can be drawn between these different carceral initiatives of the colonial port city over the centuries, it also makes sense to draw distinctions between different periods and parts of port governance rather than seeing it as an unchanging and well-integrated machine.

Books

Like all cargo, books had to pass through the protocols for becoming landed objects. Their first rite entailed moving from sea to shore, an arduous process given the weight of books and printed matter. In some cases, their mass meant they never arrived at all. In severe storms, the heaviest cargo was thrown overboard to lighten the vessel—consignments of books were an obvious choice.

If they did make it, once on land, they were subject to their next rite of passage: classification according to the tariff schedule. In South African tariff schedules of the 1910s to 1930s, books fell into the category "Books, paper and stationery."[26] The Indian tariff shared a similar classification but was more to the point, placing books under the rubric "Paper and its Applications."[27] In these schedules, books are crowded out by a demimonde of paper commodities, mainly pro forma blank documents like receipt folios, reminder slips, membership certificates, letterheads, and labels. Where books do feature, they resemble forms: account books, birthday books, Boy Scout registers, cricket score books. For Customs agents, the ideal book probably approximated a form: easily legible, readily surveyable, designed for rapid use rather than extended reading, free from any taint of sedition or obscenity. Or, as Lisa Gitelman points out in her history of the document, the form is something to be "used . . . but not authored or read."[28]

Most books passed smoothly through the system, becoming landed commodities without their containers ever being opened. When books were suspect in some way, they were stopped for inspection, where one more ritual awaited, namely, being "read." Tax collectors at heart, Customs officers were reluctant readers who regarded the inside of any book as beyond their job description. Instead, they treated publications as a form of miniature cargo—their outer covering was perused for logistic inscriptions, their inside subjected to the same protocols of measuring, sampling, and counting deployed on other troublesome consignments. Customs officers assayed books rather than read them.[29] If deemed objectionable in some way, books had their covers removed or portions of text blacked out, being then allowed to proceed as radically revised editions. In other instances, offending volumes were "unlanded," returned to the water from which they had come or sacrificed to another element, like fire.

These methods of reading by rapid scanning and sampling were reproduced in the manuals and handbooks that Customs officials used as part of their jobs—volumes to be consulted but not read in detail. This use is encoded in their layout and arrangement: some Customs manuals start with an index rather than a table of contents.[30] While the latter gives an overview of the entire book, setting out a sequence that the ideal reader will follow, an index, by contrast, separates text from table.[31] Having the index up front announces that the book is something to be consulted rather than read in toto. The manuals' status as workaday books is also apparent from the waterproof covers that generally encased such volumes and from the blank pages, either interleaved or included at the end, for taking notes.[32]

These handbooks constituted one of several genres of the dockside that took shape around incoming cargo, as already noted. With titles like *Clements' Customs Pocket Manual*, *The Tariff Dictionary: A Compendious Handbook to the Fiscal Question*, or *The Calcutta Customs Calculation Manual*, such books comprised lists of commodities, common shipping routes, summaries of maritime and Customs law, duty charged on goods in various ports, and synoptic trade profiles of a range of countries.[33] As a compendium of commercial pathways, the manual enabled readers to compare routes for their cargo and to calculate the amount of duty involved in each. A genre of international commerce, these volumes were consulted by merchants, importers and exporters, ships' passengers, and Customs officials—in short, anyone moving commodities (or luggage) around the world or governing this mobility. The titles for these manuals included words like *guide* and *assistant*, indicating the compliant role that books were expected to play on the dockside.[34]

These modes of dockside reading produced implicit definitions of what the colonial book should be, a theme that the conclusion to this book takes up. Some of these are predictable and accord with what we know about the hierarchy of books that took shape in colonial contexts. Customs helped to create and sustain such a hierarchy: at the top stood posh volumes from the metropole, sanctified by bearing the mark of British copyright. These books were embodiments of imperial power, instruments of "civilization," and calling cards of Englishness.[35] At the opposite end were books that fell under suspicion for sedition or obscenity. These books were treated as epidemiological objects, a pattern that helped lay the basis for models of censorship and gained an afterlife in library practices of fumigating books that had spent time in infected households.[36] In colonial contexts, books were relatively rare commodities, as opposed to newspapers and periodicals. Customs practices of elevation or demotion helped cement the book as a potent object, an orientation reinforced by Christian mission practices that invested the book with evangelical charisma.[37]

Another self-evident way in which the Custom House defined books was by specifying genre as an effect of the tariff schedule: in Canada novels were admitted duty-free, and duty-free books could well become novels, while in South Africa an extra 5 percent duty was levied on "paper-covered" books like comics, magazines, and dime novels, consigning these to one category, namely, dangerous trash.[38]

Beyond these well-known outcomes, Customs practices consolidated less predictable definitions of the book. These arose from the two preponderant and related modes of printed matter on the dockside, namely, the book-as-form and the handbook. Whether a diary or school register, the book-as-form offered one unwitting model of colonial writing in which a template from the metropolis was filled with local scribblings—quite literally a case of form over content. Many colonial novels followed a similar pattern, with a generic blueprint from the imperial center filled with provincial content. Such texts established colonial authorship as bland and safe, avoiding the challenge of creating something new in a situation where the colony could only ever be a copy of the metropole.

At a less abstract level, the book-as-form took on a concrete existence in settler and immigrant handbooks, which included the forms to be completed on arrival.[39] These fusions of handbook and form helped to "land" immigrants, guiding them through disembarkation formalities and making them legal. These volumes acted in concert with the port infrastructure and its land reclamation, which quite literally reached out to incoming passengers of the right class and race, giving them their first purchase on the colony. We might think of these settler handbooks-with-form as a mode of textual land reclamation or landfill, extending literary infrastructure outward to enable the immigrant to become landed.[40]

The handbook form as a genre of the dockside can usefully be inserted into discussions on southern African literature and the postcolonial novel more generally. The genre stands midway between two key colonial narrative modes: the story of the shipwreck and the farm novel. While promoting the romance of maritime manliness, the shipwreck narrative simultaneously testified to the uncertainty of the imperial venture itself. As Michael Titlestad's work indicates, shipwrecks and the stories about them called port and harbor development into being as a way of obviating further disasters at sea.[41] In some instances, actual shipwrecks close to the coast were used as the basis for land reclamation, the submarine remains being filled with stones to create a foothold for artificially extending the coastal terrain. The port and its infrastructure sought to overwrite the shipwreck. As part of this infrastructure, the genres of the dockside, like the Customs manual and settler handbook, played their part, creating a textual landfill to enable settlers to become landed and to gain traction on the colony itself. The institution through which many settlers ultimately achieved this aim was the farm, and as J. M. Coetzee has famously argued, the farm novel in turn became an important intellectual instrument of land possession and dispossession.⁴² As the conclusion argues, we might usefully think of this narrative mode as linked to the genres of the dockside.

Reading

Customs officials have always been considered ham-handed readers, and in most quarters they get a bad press. Literary representations are unforgiving, with officers portrayed as gruff (*Villette*, 1853), grim (Thomas Hardy's smuggler's tale "The Distracted Preacher," 1879), or egregious (Evelyn Waugh's *Vile Bodies*, 1930).⁴³ In the last novel, a cloddish examiner at Dover lights on a copy of Dante: "'French, eh??' he said . . . 'and pretty dirty, too.'"⁴⁴ Nathaniel Hawthorne's famous preface to *The Scarlet Letter* equally depicts the Custom House as a philistine domain where he can find little "lettered intercourse" among his colleagues, more devoted to snoozing and sinecures than to Shakespeare. Hawthorne was himself a short-lived surveyor at Salem, relieved of his political appointment by a change of regime in 1849, and his Custom House is the nemesis of literary ambition. In a much-analyzed passage, he ruefully remarks that, as a surveyor, his name would no longer be emblazoned on the title pages of books but would now be stenciled onto pepper bags and cigar boxes "in testimony that these commodities had paid the impost." He continues, "Borne on such queer vehicles of fame, a knowledge of my existence, so far as a name conveys it, was carried where it had never been before, and, I hope, will never go again."⁴⁵

In Hawthorne's calculation, the realm of the title page with a named author stands in stark opposition to the world of brute commodities in which the Custom House deals. The Custom House is inimical to literature itself. The manuscript setting out the circumstances of the scarlet letter that the narrator stumbles upon has to be removed from the Custom House and reworked before it can become a work of literature with a title page. In the Custom House, reading and writing are portrayed as limited and mechanical. The manuscript has been prepared by the hand of a previous surveyor and lists only the barebones facts; it needs rewriting to become literary. As Patricia Crain points out, when the narrator first encounters the fabric scrap of the scarlet letter, he approaches it as a surveyor would, measuring its length, each "limb" "three-and-a-half inches." Yet, to elevate himself into the realm of literature with a capital L, Hawthorne has to abandon the quantifying methods of the Custom House and "stamps his name on the A claiming with magisterial confidence the story of its origin as his own," thereby returning his name to the title page.⁴⁶ Drawing on Meredith McGill's incisive analysis that shows Hawthorne repositioning himself from a provincial and popular writer to a national figure, we can read his disavowal of the Custom House as part of this pattern.[47]

In short, for Hawthorne, the title page as a sign of inspired and individual authorship is entirely at odds with the corporate stupor and mechanical methods of the Custom House. The title page and Custom House occupy discrete circuits of value that should never intersect. Yet these two domains did overlap when Customs officials had occasion to scrutinize title pages. In these forms of reading, the name on the title page and the initials on the commodity become more or less equivalent. Both are logistic metadata intended to aid the passage and circulation of the object on which they appear. As the philistine reputation of Customs indicates, these modes of reading have invariably been treated as scandalous and outrageous. Nadine Gordimer's description of the South African censorship board (which in part grew out of Customs censorship) is apposite: in a letter of protest to the apartheid state written in 1973, she observed that censors treated literature "as a commodity to be boiled down to its components and measured like a bar of soap."[48]

Writing in the 1970s from the depth of apartheid South Africa, Gordimer mobilizes a humanist ideal of literary creation against the growing juggernaut of censorship, a move entirely understandable given the dark era from which she spoke. From this perspective, reading literature like a bar of soap can only be a sign of brutish antihumanism. Yet, as we move into a posthumanist, object-oriented, and digital age, literature is already being read like a bar of soap. In the realm of digital literary criticism, reading by metadata and algorithmic selection is routine. In massive corpus analyses, the text itself is not intended for the literary critic but rather for the algorithm, which will select appropriate portions. Such procedures are not far removed from the Custom House, where examiners read by metadata, did not regard themselves as the addressees of the texts, and proceeded by sampling rather than reading the text in its entirety. The Customs inspector and the algorithm have more in common than first meets the eye. Indeed, as others have argued, bureaucratic reading pretends to be algorithmic, universal, and dispassionate in its application while bureaucrats like to think of themselves as virtual machines, sitting atop the hardware of rules and procedures.[49]

Customs officials took a deflationary attitude toward books, an approach that dovetails with current book history methods that seek to unseat the codex from its humanist pedestal. Customs officials were more interested in the book's material substrate than its textual interior and treated books as but one item among many. Book historians follow similar "detexting" methods, tracing practices of not-, non-, half-, or semireading: recycling the book as paper, presenting it as a calling card more discussed than read, or trying to sidestep the laborious nature of reading by speeding it up.[50] To this list, we can add the epidemiological reading method of the Custom House in which text is imagined as a cloud of pathogens so that the reader wants as little exposure as possible to the book, a mode of reading that was to have a long afterlife in censorship practices. Another strategy was to speed up reading by sampling or by treating it as a mechanized activity. When inspectors perused one book, they were not simply dealing with a singular volume; they were reading the whole consignment, or even edition, treating the book as the industrially mass-produced commodity it was (and is).

Yet the more examiners demediated the book or treated it as uncooperative stationery, the more it doggedly asserted its textual being. There are of course many circumstances in which a book's textual nature can be happily ignored as it is repurposed to line drawers or pie dishes. Yet the hydrocolonial frontier was not one of these. As books crossed from land to sea, if suspect in any way, their wordy interiors demanded attention. Just as tea had to be sniffed and alcohol gauged, books had to be read. Customs officials tried to get around this reality but in the end had to accommodate themselves to the book as textual object, formulating methods of dockside reading as a compromise, an uneasy settlement shaped as much by the book itself as by the inspector.

The Custom House realigned the elements of the book, emphasizing its outer markings at the expense of its inner content—a type of texternalization.[51] This realignment took shape in the elemental environment of the port, occasioning redefinitions of what the book could or should be. The reading methods of the Custom House can hence be described as elemental, a topic that leads us to hydrocolonialism, the rubric under which such elemental reading is best discussed.

Hydrocolonialism

This book investigates shore-shaped methods of reading that crystallized around the Custom House and raises larger questions of literary formations across land and sea. The term *hydrocolonialism* is proposed as a conceptual framework for these themes.[52]

A neologism, *hydrocolonialism* riffs off the term *postcolonialism* and, like that concept, has a wide potential remit that could include colonization by way of water (various forms of maritime imperialism), colonization of water (occupation of land with water resources, the declaration of territorial waters, the militarization and geopoliticization of oceans), a colony on (or in) water (the ship as a miniature colony or a penal island), colonization through water (flooding of occupied land), and colonization of the idea of water (establishing water as a secular resource).[53] While the word *hydrocolonialism* is an invention, two related uses are encountered on the web. The first is *hydrocolony*, a Canadian term for a workers' housing development near a hydroelectric plant. The second is a grammatically incorrect synonym for *hydrocolonic*, that is, colonic irrigation, which at times appears as *hydrocolonial irrigation*. Both of these raise pertinent themes: the first points to the "fundamental connection between water, its management, and the colonial or neocolonial relations in the modern era," as Sara Pritchard argues in her account of hydroimperialism in Algeria.[54] Designating the workers' housing development as a colony speaks of an imperial imaginary in the management of water and the labor associated with it. Hydroelectric dams are showpieces of modernity, displacing communities and affecting aquatic ecologies and river flows. The hydrocolony consequently speaks to themes of colonial control and environmental degradation. The term *hydrocolonial/hydrocolonic irrigation* resonates with these themes by suggesting accelerated processes of waste making. However erroneous the term, it captures metaphorically the waste-making systems of colonial rule, where certain people were rendered as waste, whether through the slave trade, indenture, or penal transportation. The ocean itself functions as a dumping ground for the bodies of drowned slaves and other forced migrants.

One may of course ask whether we need the term *hydrocolonialism*. It has long been appreciated that water is centrally implicated in imperial and other social orders. Water sculpts political authority, whether in the ancient hydraulic empires of Central Asia, the water dynasties of South India, the rainmaking chieftaincies of southern Africa, or the modernist hydrologic projects of the colonial and postcolonial world.[55] Geographers and anthropologists have thickened understandings of water as an "informed material" implicated in hydronationalism, struggles around citizenship, settler hydrologies, and hydrocosmologies.[56] The classic hydrologic cycle of evaporation, condensation, rainfall, and runoff has been widened to become the hydrosocial cycle. This configuration tracks how H_2O becomes the social substance water, shaped as much by capital as by contours.[57] Dilip da Cunha and Anuradha Mathur have freed the hydrologic cycle from the fiction of neatly divided land and water. Working with a monsoon context, they demonstrate "an ecosystem that is neither land nor water but one of ubiquitous wetness in which rain is held in soil, aquifers, glaciers, snowfields, building materials, agricultural fields, air, and even plants and animals." They depict a world where water is "precipitating, seeping, soaking, evaporating, and transpiring in ways that defy delineation."[58]

While these rich bodies of work are crucial to understanding sociologies of water, they do not specifically address literary concerns. Modeling itself on postcolonial theory with its cultural remit, hydrocolonialism explores the literary implications opened up by overlaying the hydrologic cycle onto imperial and postimperial cartographies. This move requires us to think laterally, vertically, and contrapuntally between different water worlds and hydroimaginaries while exploring how such circuits have been or may be narrativized. There is now an exciting repertoire of scholarship exploring these themes: critical oceanic studies, coastal and hydrocritical approaches, elemental and atmospheric methods (of which more later). Together these fields have established water as a method for doing postcolonial literary criticism. While this is too extensive to discuss exhaustively, I sketch three pertinent trends across these various fields, which for the sake of convenience I dub high, middle, and low.

In the first trend, mega- or mesoscale meteorological patterns like monsoons and cyclones or hurricanes offer ways of defining literary regions and generic structures. Most obvious in this regard is the monsoon zone of the Indian Ocean world, now an analytic matrix to track multiple networks of cosmopolitan exchange.[59] From a literary perspective, the monsoon Indian Ocean provides a method for constituting genealogies, in the anglophone domain centered on Amitav Ghosh's masterful travelogue *In an Antique Land: History in the Guise of a Traveler's Tale*, which looks back to Conrad's Indian Ocean texts and forward to writers such as the British-Zanzibari novelist Abdulrazak Gurnah and the Mauritian Lindsey Collen.[60] Particularly in Ghosh's work, the monsoon Indian Ocean is given an ideological inflection as the "third world" ocean, in which the early cosmopolitanism of the Indian Ocean arena is interrupted by European imperialisms, in turn giving rise to anti-imperial networks. Ghosh's later novels *Sea of Poppies* (2008) and *River of Smoke* (2011) create a subaltern sea of characters drawn together in a miniature, maritime Afro-Asian front. In a related vein, Collen's novel *Mutiny* constitutes the cyclone as disruptive of post/imperial infrastructures and social hierarchies (somewhat akin to flood narratives, whether in Lincolnshire or the Mississippi delta).[61]

The architecture of these formations, like the spiral or the eye, is used biomimetically to illuminate literary structures. In a long tradition of Caribbean ecopoetics, the spiral of the hurricane informs a Haitian literary movement of the 1960s, known as *spiralism*. As Kaiama Glover indicates, the spiral, whether in DNA or the Milky Way, constitutes a building block of existence while providing "a primal point of relation to a world beyond the claustrophobia and creative asphyxiation of François Duvalier's totalitarian state." She continues, "On a formal, literary level, the spiral's perfectly balanced maintenance of the centrifugal and centripetal offers a neat allegory of the tension between insular boundedness and global intention that marks [the] work."[62]

We might read these various literary texts, taken together, as imaginative interventions into the hydrosocial cycle itself. Rather like African ritual specialist rainmakers who intercede in the hydrologic cycle via the ancestors, literary texts intervene in our understanding of the water cycle and its narrative possibilities.[63] Sarah Nuttall has extended this point in her analysis of "pluvial time," examining "rainfall in and as climate crisis, and what temporal logics and narrative forms this is producing."[64]

Descending to our next level—the middle—we arrive at the coast, the site of human evolution itself and hence one of the most enduring and productive artistic terrains.[65] Postcolonial literary critics have variously analyzed the littoral as an ecotone, a place of "fractal multiplicity" and amphibiousness, which writers use to complicate orthodoxies of all sorts.[66] As Meg Samuelson indicates, "Littoral literature and coastal form ... muddle the inside-outside binary that delineates nations and continents, and which has been particularly stark in framing Africa in both imperial and nativist thought."[67] Coastal morphology and its associated water formations, or "waterside chronotopes" in Margaret Cohen's formulation, like lagoon, estuary, delta, shoal, white water, and brown water, constitute literary microregions.[68] As climate change increasingly buffets coastlines, these regions—like the Ganges-Brahmaputra delta, the Lagos lagoon, or the Bombay archipelago—become more prominent, producing narratives of coastal life and its perilous terraqueous futures.[69]

Below the waterline, the categories of oceanography that designate the different "layers" of the ocean (epipelagic, mesopelagic, abyssopelagic, and hadopelagic) are being deployed by literary scholars as engagement with the sea becomes more material and concrete. Stacy Alaimo and Joshua Bennett have both deployed the idea of violet/black, the dominant color spectrum of the abyssopelagic zone.[70] The imagination in Derek Walcott's famous "The Sea Is History" is largely epipelagic since formations and objects in the water are generally visible.[71] Given that his home island, Saint Lucia, perches on a volcanic shelf, this is perhaps to be expected. Other strands of Caribbean aesthetics, such as work by M. NourbeSe Philip or Aimé Césaire, invoke deeper formations—the volcanic, the tectonic, and the basin—and so direct our attention deeper.[72] Charne Lavery has developed these ideas in relation to the Indian Ocean, exploring the layers of the "vertical ocean" in cultural and literary terms.[73]

One important dimension of postcolonial theory has been the imperative to move away from colony/metropole binaries and to trace multidirectional empire-wide interactions. Hydrocolonialism explores these considerations contrapuntally in relation to water. As Pritchard's work on French hydrology demonstrates, hydraulic expertise built up by French engineers in French North Africa was imported back home and used to improve the techniques of "backward" provincial farmers.[74] Likewise, as Erik Swyngedouw indicates in his analysis of twentieth-century Spanish hydrohistory, the country's arid environment was characterized as "African," the outcome of peasant ignorance, a "turning back of these colonial environmental imaginaries onto the European center."[75] In literary terms, one could take an empire-wide view of moral and social hydrology that saw surplus populations as stagnant sources of contamination needing to be channeled, drained, and carried away.[76] Themes of drainage, hydrology, and flow dynamics could be read contrapuntally across empire, focusing on themes like tidal circulation in *Great Expectations* (1861) and crosshatching these with Namwali Serpell's recent novel *The Old Drift*, which draws together settler hydrologies and hydrocosmologies on the Zambezi.[77]

Together these techniques add water, depth, and verticality, extending land-focused and horizontal purviews. In a postcolonial context where land has been overdetermined and the sea overerased, such relativizing methods become especially pertinent. Land is favored both as an automatic platform of knowledge and as a locus of the colonial and anticolonial nation. The ocean, by contrast, has been forgotten, first by the emerging settler colonial nation attempting to erase its origins and then by anticolonial nationalism turning its back on the ocean as the source of imperialism. In a postnational age, the rich and creolized meanings of the ocean, both precolonially and colonially, are starting to be more systematically explored.[78] In a comparative spirit, *Dockside Reading* brings these perspectives to the emerging debates on oceanic, coastal, and elemental methods, providing a perspective from southern Africa and the Indian Ocean, to complement the North Atlantic, Caribbean, and Pacific perspectives that currently lead the way.

The various bodies of work I have set out thus far are literary critical in orientation. The primary focus of this book is on print culture and book history (although the conclusion of this book raises the question of literary genre). We turn now to consider what a hydrocolonial lens brings to these fields.

Hydrocolonial Print Cultures

A hydrocolonial approach makes visible the mutually shaping relationship between print culture and the elemental politics of the colonial maritime frontier. It enables us to configure printed matter, colony, and ocean in ways that establish a more dynamic relationship among these three terms. This triad of print, ocean, and colony has certainly been explored in the rich research on printed matter and maritime circulation. This work has, however, largely proceeded in a "dry" register with the sea as a backdrop. Scholars have followed printed matter out to sea, tracing what Atlantic sailors read and wrote and how their shipboard activities shaped literary representations of the ocean.[79] Ships were textual machines (or "floating secretariats") that transported and produced vast numbers of documents and publications.[80] Books and publications were dotted across the ship: in the hold as cargo, in the captain's cabin as parcels, with sailors, with passengers, in ships' libraries.[81] Passengers themselves produced newspapers on board and scribbled poetry.[82] This scholarship suggests that this circulation produced a range of literary subject positions, whether shipboard identities, diasporic alignments, imperial loyalties, or colonial nationalist formations.

Hydrocolonialism takes a different tack, putting water and paper closer together, immersing printed matter in the elemental politics of the colonial port city. The burgeoning field of elemental media studies provides a useful framework for this purpose. As Nicole Starosielski indicates, "All media becomes environmental media, and all media studies becomes environmental media studies," while Derek McCormack urges us to trace the continuities "between entities and the elemental conditions in which these entities are immersed and in which they participate."[83] As John Durham Peters suggests, the elements themselves have come to be understood as "infrastructures of being" and "agencies of order."[84] As we have seen, printed matter was implicated in defining the elements, notably "the land" and the "anti-environment" of the ocean.[85] By becoming landed, printed matter affirmed colonial possession of the port city, while books that were "unlanded" designated the ocean as a place of disposal. Dry aspects of print culture like censorship became elementally implicated, with water being used as a medium of expurgation. British copyright, too, became embroiled in the elemental frontier of the colony, acting as a sign of propriety and a clearance for the book to become fully landed.

When applied to print culture on the dockside, a hydrocolonial method highlights printed matter as part of port infrastructure, both in terms of the manuals and forms that officials used and in terms of these as types of virtual land reclamation or landfill. Such an approach extends our attention underwater to focus on the submarine infrastructure and engineering that enabled the port in the first instance. Printed matter can be connected to the water and submarine infrastructure around it—entities and elemental conditions are made continuous. Jesse Oak Taylor's observation on atmospheric thinking, while looking more up than down, is apposite: "Atmospheric thinking emphasizes adjacency; it considers the way that bodies of all kinds influence the conditions of possibility in their vicinity."[86] A hydrocolonial method makes the Custom House and its object contiguous with the elements of the port city. This adjacency produces two important themes: colonization of water and creolization of water.

COLONIZED WATER Central to hydrocolonial thinking is how water comes to be colonized. Siobhan Carroll's work on elements and empire is instructive in this regard, showing how air, water, and ice initially appeared uncolonizable and empire-proof, largely because they could not be settled or occupied.[87] In the longer run, these elements were indeed rendered colonizable, whether as sites of performing imperial masculinity, as resources to be extracted, as dumping grounds for waste, or as methods of defining or redefining international law and geopolitics.[88] The long-term effectiveness of these strategies is apparent today if we turn to the ocean, which from its seabed to its surface has been prospected, militarized, mined, and laid claim to, as Elizabeth DeLoughrey has recently pointed out. As she indicates, a hydrocriticism for the twenty-first century needs to engage less with "the concepts of fluidity, flow, routes, and mobility [than with] less poetic terms such as blue water navies, mobile offshore bases, high-seas exclusion zones, sea lanes of communication (SLOCs), and maritime 'choke points.'" She advocates a shift from hydrocriticism to hydropower that can take account of "larger geopolitical and geontological (or sea-ontological) shifts."[89]

In southern Africa, coastal waters around port cities were colonized through "aquatic territorialism."[90] Through this, land was extended into the sea, either literally through reclamation and submarine infrastructure or by the extension of land-based methods of governance over the ocean: promulgations of sovereignty, port regulations pertaining to the intertidal zone, declarations of quarantine stations over areas around ships.[91]

Port cities contrive possession, of water and sediment as much as of dry land. As an antidote to the shipwreck, port engineering becomes a central narrative of colonial possession and a founding mythology of port cities themselves. The harbor engineer becomes a minor imperial figure, a tireless soldier who takes on the Sisyphean battle against sand. Yet the prominence of these narratives is short-lived as colonial possession moves inland and the sea recedes into the distance. Dredging, after all, is not easily mythologized. This submarine imperialism is only starting to find a conceptual vocabulary. Ben Mendelsohn's work on Lagos offers an instructive example that demonstrates how "sand and related coastal geomorphological processes interact with the city's political and imaginative trajectories as well as its historical legacies."[92]

Chapter 1 touches on this submarine engineering and, in so doing, engages with a vibrant body of critical oceanic studies that shifts away from older surface-oriented approaches and engages with the materiality of the sea by going below the waterline. One strand in this scholarship relativizes land-based epistemologies via the ocean. Terming these "dry technologies," this work immerses concepts and theories to produce new modes of analysis.[93] Whether based on actual diving experience, analytic immersion, the act of "thinking with" species, or submarine aesthetics, this work traces how, by what media and genres, and with what effects the unseen ocean is mediated to human audiences.[94] Critics adumbrate how these forms—whether speculative fiction, underwater photography, aquariums, rococo decoration, shipwrecks, coral reefs, or conceptual poetry—mediate the undersea and how they deal with representational problems of scale, depth, and visibility.[95]

While this book is largely located at, or on, the waterline, it draws attention to underwater sites as places of analytic possibility, tracing how these are mediated physically through submarine infrastructure and metaphysically through the spiritual congregations that assemble there in what I call *creolized water*.

CREOLIZED WATER As many rich studies have taught us, port cities are intense nodes of cosmopolitan exchange. These historiographies have, however, largely kept their eyes on land, an orientation that *Dockside Reading* shifts by directing our view offshore and, briefly, underwater. This perspective builds on work I have done elsewhere on Durban, while drawing on an emerging method that uses the harbor floor as a site to explore port cities from a submarine perspective. My particular investigation speculated on what kind of remains might have accumulated in Durban harbor and its hintersea.[96] In addition to shipwrecks, collapsed infrastructure, and detritus dumped by ships and port workers (including books thrown into the ocean by Customs officials), there would also have been traces that speak to the cosmopolitanism of the port city. These would have included the paraphernalia of Hindu-Muslim religious festivals that were immersed in the ocean.[97] These remnants in turn remind us of the variety of oceanic imaginaries to be found in any port city. In the case of Durban, these could have included maritime mythologies from South Asian groups, Zulu speakers, and African dockworkers from further afield, as well as port officials drawn from across the world. Speculating on and from the Durban harbor floor redefines water itself as cosmopolitan or creolized, containing both the material and imaginative remains of different communities around the port city.

While true for any body of water, such creolization would be especially pertinent in imperial and postimperial settings. Southern African waters, for example, are especially creolized, being the imagined domain of African ancestors, Khoisan ("first nation") water spirits and deities, and Muslim water jinn associated with enslaved communities brought to the Cape under the Dutch, as well as imperial ideals of maritime manliness.[98]

The concept of creolized water can usefully be put into conversation with Black hydropoetics and the Middle Passage. Ancestral and "aquafuturist" (to use Suzanna Chan's term), a body of creative and scholarly explorations experiment with the Atlantic undersea as a realm of speculative diasporic histories.[99] Notable examples include Ellen Gallagher's mixed-media explorations of the Black Atlantic submarine, the meditations of Christina Sharpe on the molecular remains of enslaved bodies and their "residence time," and the electronic music of Drexciya and the underwater realm it imagines, where the children of drowned captives have adapted to submarine living.[100] Together these constitute Black hydropoetics as a major focus of diasporic scholarship and constitute the undersea as a potent source of ancestral memory and imagination.

Putting Black hydropoetics in relation to southern African creolized water opens up suggestive submarine cartographies. These might map how southern African oceanic ancestral traditions relate to the drowned communities of both the Atlantic and Indian Oceans, the arena from which Cape slaves were drawn.[101] Once one considers this enlarged realm, the dramatis personae expand, taking in the jinn and genies of the Indian Ocean, the ancestors of the African oceans, the submerged deities of Indian indentured communities, and the drowned of both the Middle Passage and the Indian Ocean.

The Custom House was involved in both the colonization and creolization of water. As indicated, Custom Houses were located on unstable coastal terrain and were subject to the vagaries of the ocean, as job titles in the Customs service, like tide waiter, tide surveyor, beach magistrate, and receiver of wrecks, indicate. Customs officials were eager participants in debates on how best to engineer the port and extend its footprint into the ocean. We might describe them as a *hydrocracy*, ruling by and from the water's edge rather than from the desk of bureaucracy.

In undertaking this work, Customs officials nurtured cosmologies that fed into the hydroimaginaries of the ocean. Like much colonial thinking, these ideas were starkly dichotomized, with the sea defined, on the one hand, as a dumping ground for contaminated goods and, on the other, as the realm of naval heroism and seafaring manliness. The practice of dumping condemned goods instituted what was to become a long-standing technique of colonial governance, namely, using water as a site of erasure and in some cases execution—in the Dutch empire, those convicted of sodomy were in some instances sentenced "to be taken out to sea, thrown overboard and drowned."[102] In the twentieth century, the apartheid and Pinochet regimes routinely dumped the corpses of murdered political prisoners at sea.[103] During the period of decolonization, departing colonial regimes, especially in the Caribbean, regularly tipped incriminating documentation into the ocean.[104]

As regards the second view of the ocean, Customs officials were great admirers of the navy, whose uniforms, terminology, insignia, and hierarchies they mimicked. Customs officials deployed this naval mystique on land to buttress their authority and to present themselves as an officer class. Epauletted and brass-buttoned, the Customs officers formed a congregation of white men who attempted to separate themselves from the cosmopolitan cacophony of the port city. The singing of Zulu stevedores was abjured; Madrassi oarsmen who steered *masulah* boats through the surf to ships in the roadstead were ignored. The archival records of Customs create the impression that the officers inhabited a whites-only world. Only the odd job title like "native messenger" and "female typist" and architectural drawings showing segregated toilet facilities indicate otherwise.[105]

Structure of the Book

The introduction has focused on dockside reading as a site of hydrocoloniality. The remainder of the book explores this intersection in five steps: (1) the history of colonial Customs and its hydrocolonial modes of governance; (2) the interaction of Customs regimes of identification, objects, and environments; (3) copyright; (4) censorship; and (5) the way dockside reading shaped colonial authorship and literary genres. The substance of the chapters on copyright and censorship may seem drier, or less obviously hydrocolonial, than the other chapters. Yet the influence of the colonial maritime frontier is present in two ways. First, both chapters trace how epidemiological anxieties that originated with the ship as a potential vector of disease modulated into ideological imperatives of boundary making and exclusion that in turn shaped practices around copyright and censorship. Second, both chapters open on or near the waterfront, a reminder that this was the setting in which Customs examiners worked.

The details of each chapter are as follows. Chapter 1 sketches out the histories of English Customs and then colonial Customs in southern Africa (and other parts of the empire). This account is focused largely around one man, George Rutherford, who made his career in London, Kingston (Jamaica), Saint George's (Grenada), and Durban. In tracing his professional biography, the chapter describes the culture of colonial Customs and its modes of hydrocolonial governance. These entailed the extension of territorial forms of sovereignty to coastal waters while bringing quasi-naval modes of authority onto land. A coda to this chapter makes a brief foray underwater to think about the submarine infrastructure that kept the Custom House standing and gave its personnel a purchase on imperial mythologies of the sea. This harbor development adversely affected other communities' access to and imagination of the ocean, diminishing the creolization of the coastal waters.

Chapter 2 starts with a Customs scene, set on a beach in a small port in the Cape Colony. An image from the *Illustrated London News* shows goods being landed from a lighter by porters who wade through the water while a landing waiter on the beach tallies the cargo. The chapter uses this image as a starting point to explore Customs procedures and protocols, highlighting how their rituals of identification were shaped by the maritime environments and the objects with which they dealt.

Chapter 3 opens on board ship with passengers sorting their books before entering port. In some parts of the empire, reprints of British copyrighted works were not permitted and had to be tossed overboard. However, no one, let alone Customs officials, was entirely sure what the legal situation actually was, since different, contradictory levels of copyright legislation existed: imperial, colonial, and international. In attempting to deal with this confusion, examiners hewed to their everyday practice and the logic of the cargo mark, relying heavily on the Merchandise Marks Act of 1887, which dealt with trade descriptions and marks of origin ("made in England," "made in Australia," etc.) and construed copyright as an "indirect sign of manufacture." Under these circumstances, copyright became a poor semiotic cousin to the mark of origin and, in cases of British copyright, a sign of propriety that the object had been made in

Britain and was hence respectable and implicitly "white." This latter practice was shaped by the ideological exigencies of a hydrocolonial boundary, which were translated into an epidemiological register, embroiling copyright in the elemental politics of the port city. The chapter traces how copyright played out beyond the port and concludes by discussing how these colonial instances feed into current debates on copyright.

Chapter 4 briefly shifts location and begins on the dockside of Sydney Harbour with two lowly Customs officials stuck in a small, hot office, hankering after the sea but required to leaf through piles of publications looking for signs of obscenity. The chapter explores how Customs officers like these two men dealt with undesirable publications. Tax collectors rather than readers, they "read" logistically by scanning metadata, sampling, and counting. These object-oriented modes of reading extend our understandings of censorship, which tend to look higher up the bureaucratic chain and to assume that censors read everything placed in front of them. The chapter focuses on two moments: the first is the South African War (Anglo-Boer War) of 1899–1902, when Customs took on a major role censoring and banning pro-Boer material. The second shifts to the 1920s and 1930s, a period of growing anticommunism. This mixture of military-style censorship and anticommunism laid the groundwork for a style of logistic reading that informed subsequent apartheid censorship regimes. Running through these various modes of censorship is a strong epidemiological strand, a reminder of the shaping influence of the colonial maritime setting and its hydrocolonial imperatives.

The conclusion explores the implications of these Customs reading regimes beyond the port. It examines the various models of the book that dockside reading produced and the implications of these for ideas of colonial authorship. These themes are traced at the level of literary genres, drawing out the relationships among the shipwreck narrative, port-city genres, and the farm novel. The analysis focuses on two texts: J. Forsyth Ingram's settler and merchant handbook, *The Story of an African Seaport: Being the History of the Port and Borough of Durban, the Seaport of Natal* (1899), and Olive Schreiner's *The Story of an African Farm* (1883).

1

The Custom House and
Hydrocolonial Governance

Customs and Excise is an obscure and little-studied institution. The red and green lanes in the airport remind us that they're there, and we might have encountered Customs officials as B-grade detectives in novels and films about drug smuggling, but we have little idea of how they work in practice.[1] This is especially true in relation to colonial Customs establishments, about which we know even less, except in cases like the United States and Ireland, where the Custom House became an anti-imperial flash point.[2] This chapter approaches the story of colonial Customs through George Rutherford, who made his career first in London, then the British West Indies, and, finally, Natal, where he was collector of customs from 1854 to 1889. Through Rutherford, the chapter explores colonial Customs as a hydrocolonial formation, paying attention to its imbrication in imperial structures and to the littoral conditions in which it operated. In a concluding coda, we go underwater to consider the submarine infrastructures that propped up the Custom House and gave its officials and their ideas purchase on the ocean, enabling them to sideline the oceanic practices and imaginaries of other sections of Durban's cosmopolitan population.

IN TRACING A wider context of colonial Customs, William Ashworth's exemplary work on the history of Customs and Excise in England provides one starting point. As he demonstrates, Customs and Excise, a key instrument of taxation and revenue generation, has long shaped modes of governance. Customs (taxing of goods traveling over borders) is the older part of the equation, dating back to the thirteenth century, while Excise (taxing of goods within borders) is a seventeenth-century departure used to raise funds for the Parliamentary forces during the English Civil War.[3] From its inception, Customs was a feudalistic institution bristling with sinecures and perquisites. Excise, by contrast, was rapidly forced to become modern, in part because it was so widely hated—excise officers had the right of search and entry, especially in relation to liquor production, making the excise man a universally reviled figure. Under close public scrutiny, excise officers had to make their procedures visible and defensible. The nature of their work (checking the composition, weight, measure, quality, and production processes of goods) promoted scientific standardization while advancing ideas of public health. These procedures standardized and policed the qualities of goods, making visible how, and with what substances, commodities had been made. As Ashworth argues, "To tax a good frequently required it to be rendered visible both in terms of its ingredients and in the way it was produced."[4]

Ashworth focuses predominantly on England and Britain, although colonial Customs appear on the horizon from time to time, especially in the lead-up to the American Revolution. Known from the seventeenth century as the "Customs Establishments in the British Plantations," these various posts fell under the London Board of Customs, to whom they reported until the repeal of the mercantilist Navigation Acts in 1849, after which Custom Houses mostly reported to the treasury of their colonial legislatures. The term *plantation*, a seventeenth-century synonym for *colony*, was initially applied to Britain's Atlantic possessions but lingered on in the terminology of the board, ironically anticipating the current use of the term. By the 1830s the Customs services of most British possessions (bar British India) reported to the board and were classified under "plantations," whether Gambia, South Australia, or New Zealand. The various plantation ports in which these Custom Houses operated varied enormously in terms of size, setting, and the local interests to which they were generally captive. Yet, these differences notwithstanding, they shared, at least in theory, some sense of being an institution apart since they reported not to the Colonial or Foreign Office (or its precursors) but to the Board of Customs. Colonial Customs regarded itself as something of an empire within an empire, a type of secular freemasonry with recondite in-house rules and symbols. These had been adopted from the byzantine and feudal practices of Customs in London and then elaborated on the mercantilist waterfronts of the first British Empire and its major commodities, slaves and sugar. Yet, even as reporting lines shifted after the end of the Navigation Acts, the older traditions of the Customs services persisted.

The career of George Rutherford straddles these shifts. Born in Hackney in 1818, he commenced his career as a young man in Her Majesty's Customs Service on the London docks. In his twenties he moved to Kingston, Jamaica, and then to Saint George's, Grenada, where he become subcollector, before relocating with his wife, Marianne Sloan, and a child to Durban in 1854.[5] In Kingston and then Saint George's, Rutherford would have encountered one of the major tasks of Customs, namely, superintending the arrival and distribution of unfree labor. He had arrived after the abolition of slavery in 1834, but even after the slave trade in the British Empire had ended in 1807, captives "liberated" from ships seized by British naval squadrons had continued to arrive in the British Caribbean.[6] Once brought to port, the "liberated Africans," as they were known, were placed in the custody of the collector, who then parceled them out as apprentices or indentured workers, inevitably to friends, family, or powerful plantation owners. After the abolition of slavery in 1834, indentured laborers from India, China, and elsewhere began arriving in the Caribbean, where they were initially placed in the custody of an official known as the protector, a position in all probability modeled on the methods of operation established by the collector of customs.

These custodial practices had first arisen during the slave trade itself when Customs officials, often themselves slaveholders, had an intimate involvement with captives: they entered ship holds to count bodies, reckoned the duty to be paid, and detained those not on the manifest.[7] Customs officials in plantation ports, notably Saint Helena, Cape Town, Mauritius, and British West African ports, undertook similar functions in relation first to slavery and then to the administration of recaptives. In the Cape Colony, where the first formal Customs arrangements were established under British occupation in 1796, the schedule of Customs fees, which included duty on slaves, was adopted from Jamaica.[8]

In Durban, Rutherford arrived in another sugar colony but one without slaves or any significant number of liberated Africans. However, debates were afoot about bringing in indentured labor from British India, with the first group arriving in 1860. Writing to his brother-in-law in 1859, Rutherford supported the use of indentured labor ("coolies"), a system he had encountered in his previous postings. He confided in his brother-in-law that this workforce would correct "an extraordinary anomaly in this colony": the Zulu population, "wealthy in flocks and herds" and occupying "vast tracts of land," resisted attempts to recruit them for plantation labor.[9] The first indentured workers arrived from Madras in November 1860, described in a local settler newspaper as "living cargo."[10] Rutherford would have been involved with processing the workers and dispatching them to sugar plantations.

OVER THE COURSE of his thirty-five-year career in the Durban port precinct, Rutherford occupied two Custom Houses. The first, built shortly before he arrived, perched forlornly behind some dilapidated wooden buildings and wharfage (figure 1.1). The second Custom House was built some twenty years later (figure 1.2). A square cupola-topped building with a neoclassical facade, it was set back from the water on reclaimed land and much-extended wharfage. These two Custom Houses usefully summarize the trajectory of colonial Custom Houses, which in their early phases were located perilously close to the sea itself. As the harbor developed, they shifted back from the waterline. Yet, even as they moved further away, Customs officials instrumentalized the elements in a form of hydrocolonial governance that extended territorial forms of governance out to sea while bringing naval modes of authority onto land.

The initial attempts to extend authority over the ocean were not especially successful. In Durban the Custom House was threatened by encroaching sea and sand, against which homemade remedies like wattle groynes, latticing, and indigenous plants used as sand cover provided only temporary relief.[11] This would have been typical of many small colonial ports, where Custom Houses were tumbledown affairs. Indeed, in some instances, the Customs post might have been mistaken for a castaway situation, comprising little more than a tent, a boat, and a flagstaff. Buildings offered scarcely more protection, since these were prone to flooding, storm surges, and, in some regions, hurricanes. Erecting

FIGURE 1.1 Durban harbor in the 1870s. The Custom House is the middle building on the right. Source: Photographic Collection on Durban, Local History Museums' Collection, Durban.

these buildings, generally on sandy soil, was a challenge: in one small Cape port, the builder complained that specialized foundations had to be triple the normal depth, while working in bad weather delayed completion.[12]

Yet, as these ports expanded and as larger Custom Houses appeared, experiments with extending landed authority over the marine environment gained momentum. Colonial sovereignty extended three nautical miles out to sea, a boundary to which the Custom House gave substance by noting the ships that crossed it (a point deemed to mark the beginning of the importation process) and by dumping decommissioned goods just beyond this boundary. These acts of disposal were carried out with considerable ceremony, with at least two officials going by boat to the three-mile mark, where they pitched rifles, perished shoes, jewelry, cigars, umbrellas, and the odd book into the ocean.[13] On their return to land, a certificate was signed to record the destruction. Each foray out to sea defined the ocean as the garbage dump of the state.

Custom Houses were legal ports of entry, and their limits and boundaries had to be defined and proclaimed, imposing land-based measurements onto

The Custom House   31

FIGURE 1.2 Durban harbor in the 1890s (about two decades after figure 1.1). The Custom House is the building in the center with the cupola. Source: Photographic Collection on Durban, Local History Museums' Collection, Durban.

coastal morphologies. A typical example from a South Australian Customs handbook defines the limits of Port Adelaide: "To extend over all the waters, creeks, and inlets embraced within . . . Port Adelaide and over one nautical league to seaward, measured from the low-watermark, on any part of the shoals or sand banks at the entrance of these creeks, waters, or inlets." Other descriptions list measurements like links, miles, and yards as well as cardinal directions and degrees, which are laid over the tidal landscapes of bays, beaches, and estuaries, all of which render precise measurement uncertain.[14]

In turn, the deploying of maritime mystique on land had a long history in the Customs service, apparent in its use of flags. The right to fly such flags dated back to the seventeenth century, when nonmilitary branches of the king's service were granted their own flag designs to distinguish them from navy vessels. Customs had a range of flags for use on land as well as pennants and ensigns for their vessels when chasing suspected smugglers. In having their own flags, Customs and Excise borrowed some of the glamour of the navy and participated in the "heraldry and traditional language of the sea."[15]

This attachment to pageantry and flags emerges in a run-in between Rutherford and the harbor engineer, who in 1878 wanted to claim fifteen feet of the Custom House frontage to build a road. Rutherford stood at the height of his powers, being both collector and chair of the Harbour Board, his department, the most prestigious in the port precinct. He dismissed the request with contempt. The space in front of the Custom House was essential to business, he insisted, and afforded a view of the waterfront.[16] In claiming this, Rutherford may have been thinking of the architecture of the mercantile waterfront, which was, as one historian notes, "the most important image of a port city, both a maritime business card and a welcome sight for travelers coming over the sea."[17] The second Custom House was the most imposing building on the Durban waterfront, and Rutherford's insistence on keeping its frontage open possibly aimed to provide incoming passengers with the requisite vista—an echo of the grand Custom Houses of the empire, whether in London, Dublin, or Calcutta, which all faced onto water and were always pictured from this vantage point. The Custom House frontage also had more practical uses when Customs officials examined packages and cargo. As the collector wrote, "It gives me authority over [the area] in the maintenance of some degree of order and quiet, necessary to the proper discharge of official business." Rutherford complained that the change would only bring the racket, and the workers associated with it, closer to his doorstep.[18]

Another reason to reject the harbor engineer's plan was that the contested area housed the Customs flagstaff. Rutherford was particularly stung by the allegation that this flagstaff was often unadorned and hence that flag etiquette had not been observed. He countered, "There has always been a public Flagstaff in front of the Custom House maintained and kept in repair by the Government for the last 20 years. . . . The usual flags—also provided by the Government are exhibited on all public and other needful occasions."[19]

Rutherford's attachment to the Custom House flag may also suggest that he understood himself to be a "flag officer," that is, senior enough to be entitled to fly a flag to mark the position from which he exercised command. Naval in origin, the term was a reminder of how senior Customs officials identified themselves as a type of navy on land, or at least an institution with a powerful seafaring orientation. Their uniforms were naval in appearance, generally dark blue with white facings and further marine touches: anchors on brass buttons and round naval caps. Their vocabulary borrowed from the maritime world. Goods were not simply abandoned but "abandoned to" the Custom House (an intransitive formulation from maritime insurance). The complex tariff calculation undertaken by Customs clerks could involve *primage*, a term originally meaning a small sum paid to a captain for extra care of cargo. Some Custom Houses provided retirement sinecures for old sea captains (an arrangement admirably captured in Nathaniel Hawthorne's preface to *The Scarlet Letter*).

Even patterns of residence for Customs officials could be determined by the comings and goings of ships. On the London docks, Customs staff were expected to live within hailing distance so that if a vessel arrived, they could be summoned, if not for all hands on deck, then at least on dock. Under Rutherford, the Durban Custom House followed similar principles, with some employees refusing to live away from the immediate port precinct. In one case, a Customs watchman, Mr. Spradbrow, turned down an offer of accommodation that involved moving half a mile away to the nearby town. Instead, he clung resolutely to the harbor, in part no doubt to remain in the largely male port precinct, like Hawthorne's Salem "a sanctuary into which womankind, with her tools of magic, the broom and the mop, has very infrequent access."[20] This overlap of workplace and residence created a strong homosocial corporate culture in colonial Custom Houses, which regularly organized themselves into sports teams and, in Natal, volunteer regiments.[21]

Yet, however much they might try to look and behave as though they were really mariners at heart, Customs officials were not. Echoing Joseph Conrad's sentiments about "shore people," most sailors reviled them as untrustworthy landsmen, the cat's-paw of the state, depriving seamen of their personal trade goods and smuggling opportunities. An eighteenth-century English tidewaiter produced a poem bemoaning his fate: "Ah me what various sorrows unabating, / Befall the man ill-fated to tide-waiting."[22] He and his poorly paid ilk faced the worst of all possible worlds. Required to stay on board ship for several days when a ship anchored in port, they were cold-shouldered by a resentful crew and, in one instance in Durban, refused food and water.[23] Yet they still faced the danger of possible shipwreck when lodged in vessels anchored in the roadstead while enjoying none of the solidarity of the seafarer.

Rutherford was not a man to avoid a fight, and another spat, this time with the Chamber of Commerce, illuminates his most deeply held views about the role of the Custom House. For their convenience, members of the chamber pushed for a radical reorganization of the Custom House and wanted to move the Long Room (clerical section) of the Custom House two miles away into the town center. Rutherford railed:

The Long Room is not a place for the mere mechanical receipt of cash in payment of certain duties—it is the "Public" "Room" where Masters of Ships, Importers and Consigning Agents, transact all the varied miscellaneous business appertaining to the Custom House and the administration of a variety of Statutes, Rules and Regulations.... The "Custom House of the Port" is a well-known and legally established phrase, and the Long Room and the Custom House in this port are as necessarily inseparable as at any of the British ports in England or the colonies.[24]

Rutherford's irascible underlining pinpoints his view of what the Custom House should be. First, it functions as the nerve center of maritime civility and information sharing in a mercantilist empire. Second, the colonial Custom House derives from the London Custom House, a link apparent from the name Long Room. The phrase itself stems from Christopher Wren's 1671 design for a new Custom House on the Thames, where the main office occupied the entire length of the imposing building.[25] Irrespective of their actual shape, the clerical sections of Custom Houses across the British Empire were universally known as "the Long Room." Rutherford's insistence on keeping his Custom House intact looks back to a previous era when Customs was its own miniature empire, policing protectionist imperial policies and raising revenue for London. He would certainly have agreed with one observer who said, "London had arisen out of the plantations and not out of England."[26]

IN SEPTEMBER 1901 Rutherford, then eighty-three and long retired, wrote to the prime minister of Natal, requesting a rough sketch of the major alterations that were being proposed for the port. "Although in the evening of my life, I still take a deep interest in everything connected to [the harbor]."[27] Rutherford had stepped down in 1889, effectively forced out by Harry Escombe (chief of the Harbour Board, attorney general, and subsequently prime minister), who successfully masterminded the linked processes of modernizing the harbor and implementing immigration-restriction procedures against "undesirables." Durban had become an important deepwater port, handling ever-increasing volumes of cargo to supply the burgeoning gold-mining city of Johannesburg in the interior. Yet, as more ships of larger tonnage arrived, they brought more passengers, many of the "wrong" class and color. Drawing on immigration-restriction policies forged elsewhere in the British Empire and the United States, the Natal colonial state began policing the color and class line with considerable ferocity.

Under Escombe, the Immigration Restriction Department implemented these policies and quickly became the most powerful player in the port, sidelining Rutherford and his Custom House. In Escombe's assessment, the collector's "conservative attachment to a state of things only suited to the early days of the Colony stands in the way of many a necessary reform."[28]

The conflict between the two men had a certain inevitability: one was a creature of the first British Empire, shaped in an imperial-plantation world; the other, a product of the second empire in its settler incarnation, a zealous colonial nationalist driven by a desire to industrialize the harbor and put racialized border controls in place. Yet, this conflict notwithstanding, the two systems—Customs and immigration restriction—also reinforced each other, strengthening the carceral traditions of the colonial port. As the immigration-restriction procedures took firmer shape, the functions of the two divisions started to blur, with the immigration authorities seizing suspect or undesirable literature from passengers. In some instances, especially in smaller ports and border posts, the two functions were combined in one person who doubled up as Customs and immigration representative.

Immigration restrictions further weaponized Customs' instrumentalization of land and sea: the latter the place of political disposal, the former the property of white settlers. One famous victim of this new system was to be Mohandas Gandhi, caught in a white vigilante agitation on his return from a trip to British India in 1899. Under the leadership of Escombe, white settler activists spread rumors that Gandhi was arranging an "Asiatic Invasion" and that he was bringing in Indian artisans to undercut the white labor market. His ship and another that happened to sail from Bombay at the same time were placed under quarantine in the harbor for three weeks. On finally being allowed to disembark, Gandhi was nearly lynched but managed to escape.[29] While Gandhi was still under quarantine in the harbor, a speaker told a raucous audience of two thousand that the "Indian Ocean was the proper place for those Indians (laughter), let them have it. They [whites] were not going to dispute their [Indian] right to the water there. But they must be careful not to give them the right to dispute the land adjoining that ocean."[30]

THE IDEA OF THE LAND as the birthright of white settlers had been rehearsed in the port on a daily basis through rituals of landing that were enabled and made more routine by land reclamation and submarine engineering. Any hydrocolonial account needs to take account of this infrastructure that undergirded the Custom House and gave it purchase on the ocean, enabling mystiques of maritime manliness to be nurtured from dry land. The history of Durban's port infrastructure has been extensively documented, telling a story focused on the sandbar at the mouth of the harbor that prevented all but vessels of the most modest draft from entering.[31] Across the latter half of the nineteenth century, any number of maritime engineers from England and Scotland were hired to solve the problem. They variously experimented with breakwaters, piers, and training walls, but it was finally dredging that removed the impediment. Over many decades, this sandbar became a submarine compulsion, a region intensely and imaginatively inhabited, through soundings, hydrographic and bathymetric charts, sketches, swimming, and even elementary forms of diving. Like all impediments to colonial progress, this saga was cast as a war. Indeed, one engineer, Edward Innes, who died on the job was likened to a soldier fallen in the battle against sand.[32]

As with any ocean setting, these ideologies of conquering the coastal waters constituted one strand in a wider set of oceanic imaginaries that together constituted a creolized space, mediating the undersea in different ways. For African societies on the eastern seaboard, the ocean was the realm of the ancestors and hence a place of pilgrimage, healing, training as a diviner, and, in versions of African Christianity, baptism.[33] For some Muslim communities, the sea harbored jinn, while Hindu creation myths about the churning ocean informed perceptions of the maritime world.

As submarine infrastructures gave imperial theologies a firmer foothold, the purchase of other "spiritscapes" on the ocean was rendered weaker.[34] Harbor development erased coastal sites that would have been points of ancestral access, characterized by "living water" that was active and moving. The Durban beachfront itself was increasingly defined as a whites-only space, limiting access to the ocean for ritual or festival purposes. By supporting the proponents of maritime manliness while also defining the ocean as an infrastructural space, harbor engineering helped sideline submarine cosmopolitanism. On land, much the same process occurred as the cosmopolitanism of the port city was brought under the control of white officials, increasingly invested in a fortified and racially stratified port. This aspect of colonial port city history has been well studied but in a historiography that generally keeps its eye on the land and humans. This chapter has attempted to make this scholarship more thoroughly hydrocolonial by suggesting that we think both above and below the waterline. Rutherford's career has offered an opportunity to combine the imperial trajectories of the Custom House with its location on and instrumentalization of the littoral.

2

Customs and Objects on a Hydrocolonial Frontier

In November 1878 the *Illustrated London News* (*ILN*) ran an image of a Customs scene in Port Elizabeth, a small port in the Cape Colony (figure 2.1). The scene unfolds on a beach where a team of porters unloads cargo from two lighters anchored in the background. Bowed down by the sacks on their heads, the porters move through the shallow water toward the beach. In the right-hand corner, a landing waiter, somewhat overdressed and surprisingly dry for someone who works on a beach, records details in a notebook. His well-pressed uniform points to a Custom House love of pomp and pageantry and further accomplishes the colonial work of emphasizing the semiclad bodies of the workers.

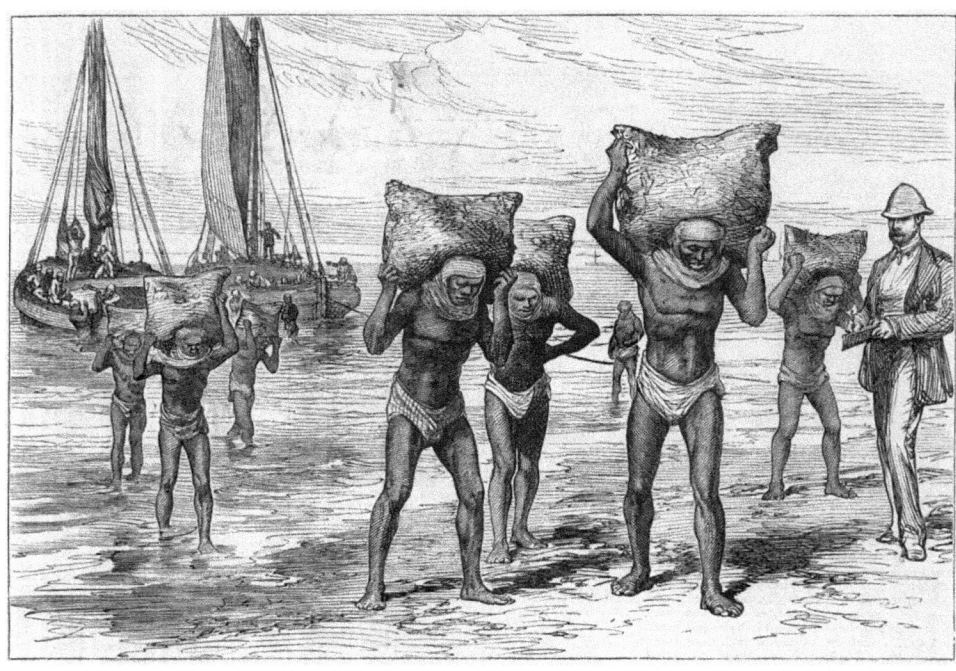

FIGURE 2.1 Landing scene, Port Elizabeth, Cape Colony. Source: *Illustrated London News*, November 23, 1878.

The waiter's literacy performs a similar task of differentiation, underlining the presumed unlettered state of the porters. Yet beyond these obvious colonial binaries lies another set of oppositions, that between sea and land, wet and dry. In contrast to the spruce landing waiter, the porters look rather like an alien, amphibious species emerging from the water, of neither the land nor the sea. This amphibiousness is accentuated by the positioning of the laborers, who appear condemned to the beach: day after day, they will carry their loads to a warehouse, then trudge back to another set of lighters.

The scene records a moment of landing, of bringing cargo to shore while subjecting it to identificatory regimes that will make it landed, that is, legally admitted. In this image the cargo is still "uncustomed" (to borrow the terminology of the Custom House) and has just begun its rites of legal and fiscal passage. In addition to formal procedures, like the tallying that the landing waiter undertakes, the process involves an instrumentalization of the elements: in this image, to be civilized is to be dry and not to have to go into the water. The cargo follows a similar trajectory, gradually attaining dryness as it moves away from the waterside and is separated from the amphibian porters who must return to the beach. The labor process of the Custom House as a whole mirrors this movement from wet to dry: jobs were classified as "waterside" or "Long Room" (clerical section), with the two terms designating an employment hierarchy—the further from the water, the higher one's status.

The *ILN* image offers an instance of dockside (or at least beachside) reading, a point at which regimes of identification intersect with objects and maritime ecologies. This chapter traces these processes in more detail, highlighting the mutually shaping interaction of these three domains.

IN THEORY, THE PROCEDURES for moving cargo from ship to wharf and then classifying it for duty purposes appear well established, with a clear set of steps, or so any number of Customs manuals indicate.[1] According to these handbooks, the "waterside" work of Customs began when any ship crossed into a three-nautical-mile zone from the coast, the point at which the process of importation was deemed to begin (export, by contrast, was complete after the cargo was twelve nautical miles out to sea). The master of the incoming vessel had twenty-four hours to present his manifest (a description of the cargo on board for that port) to the clerks in the Long Room. A tidewaiter from Customs was sent out to any ships in the roadstead to keep watch and to search for concealed cargo, whether hidden in double hulls or woven into ropes, as smuggled tobacco often was. Meanwhile, on land, the importer framed a bill of entry for his goods, estimating the amount of duty, which was then paid in the Long Room. While goods were being removed from the ship, landing waiters tallied the cargo. Examiners then cross-checked documents against the cargo, checking its marks and numbers, the quantity and sequence of cases, and the bills of entry. If satisfied, the examiner signed a delivery warrant, and the goods could proceed. If not, he detained the goods for inspection.[2]

Central to all these operations was the tariff handbook, which specified the various categories into which articles were to be assigned for purposes of duty. This process may sound fairly straightforward until one actually sees a tariff handbook, invariably a volume of some substance.[3] In the British imperial world, such handbooks hubristically promised to account for every object in the empire, if not the world, but in their very form acknowledged the impossibility of this task—tariff books were generally interleaved: every other page was blank to allow officials to write in amendments.[4]

One has only to flip through these volumes to grasp the intricacies of making such decisions. With dizzying speed, one moves from haberdashery, to haggis, to hair, from palisade fencing to pancake flour (always with the get-out clause EOHP, "except as otherwise herein provided"). Disagreements were routine, both among Customs personnel and between officials and importers keen to obtain the cheapest duty for their goods. Each such dispute generated a file, and the state archives in South Africa abound with such material as committees attempted to adjudicate how objects should be categorized. Was a young pilchard the same as a sardine? Was Gloy (a brand of bookbinding glue) the same as glue? Was there any difference between poppy seed in a packet (which could be detained under the opium laws) and poppy seed for culinary use? Fabric proved particularly tricky as officials debated whether a particular bolt of cloth should be entered as printed tartan or gingham, with swatches included.[5]

In arriving at their decisions, officials deployed different strategies of definition: exclusion (butter paper is not an "instrument, apparatus or plant"), inclusion (exhaustive lists, for example, specifying the forms that glue could take: "cakes, thin sheets, flakes, powders, crystals, pearls and in liquid form," or types of paper: blotting, brown, cartridge, drawing, handmade, manifold, packing and tissue that have "been cut, manipulated or manufactured in any way after having left the mill"), stipulation ("except as otherwise herein provided"), and ostension ("would it be straining the tariff item too far" to treat a sheep's ear tag as an "agricultural implement").[6]

While in theory the tariff schedule held taxonomic sway, the precision of these various definitions points to the role that objects themselves exerted, calling into being strings of enumerative definitions as officials sought to classify them. This "small agency" rested not only with individual objects but between objects and the environments in which they found themselves.[7]

THE *ILN* IMAGE is a useful reminder of how, in smaller ports, objects had to be wrested from their environments: in this case, first from the ship, then the lighter, followed by the beach. This work was undertaken by porters, dockworkers, and boatmen, on whom Customs officials were entirely dependent. These workers were, however, routinely screened out in Customs officials' ongoing attempt to make themselves waterproof and to distance themselves from those who labored at the water's edge. However, escape from the water was not always possible. As the previous chapter indicates, Custom Houses were not infrequently threatened by tide, flood, and surge. The coastal environment further determined how, where, and when work was done, decreeing when launches could go out to roadstead ships or shaping the style of the water- and wind-resistant hats and breeches that had to be commissioned for officers, as well as the waterproof covering of their notebooks.[8] Job descriptions like *tidewaiter, tide surveyor, landing waiter,* and *landing surveyor* reminded their holders of their dependence on time and tide, however much they might wish to dissociate themselves from the waterfront.

In more developed ports with docking facilities, discharging cargo was simpler, yet nonetheless the objects still had to be redeemed, this time from the microclimate of the hold, a fetid space, especially if poorly stowed. In such circumstances, items could "injure" each other (to use a term of maritime trade). Turpentine contaminated flour; oats heated up, melting contiguous tallow and cheese; guano blackened nuts and leather; salt buckled paper; coffee berries "readily imbibe[d] exhalations from other bodies."[9] Examiners had to decide whether the commodity, if damaged, counted as an object at all or had to be destroyed.

Customs' tracking of cargo began in such holds, where tallyers counted containers, sacks, and barrels as they were unloaded, cooperating closely with teams of stevedores who winched and then carried the cargo by hand. The leader of these longshoremen, the gangway man, gave hand signals to the winchmen, stevedores, and tallyers so that cargo could be lowered without accident.[10] Tallyers depended intimately on dockworkers, yet, going by Customs manuals, this part of the sequence appeared never to exist, with cargo being agentlessly transferred from hold to wharf.

Once discharged, most cargo passed smoothly through Customs without being opened, officials paying attention only to logistic inscriptions on its outer casing. But in about 10 percent of cases, cargo was stopped and checked. In such instances, cargo was removed from its casing for closer examination. Hence, two types of "reading" were required from Customs examiners, one that focused on exterior markings and another that required a much closer scrutiny of the object itself.

As regards the former, this style of reading entailed keeping track of the "marks and numbers," a series of inscriptions branded, painted, stenciled, or stamped on the outer casing or packaging of the cargo itself. Also known as *shipping marks* or *shipper's marks*, these code-like signs carried information like the name or symbol of the shipper, the country of origin, the sequential package number, the quantity, and the weight.

To the untutored, the marks could take a bewildering variety of forms: names, initials, numbers, circles, rectangles, and triangles. A manifest for the ship *Chelsea* carrying a general cargo from London to New York in 1828 lists eighty items. Next to each item of cargo appears its corresponding mark in the left-hand column. While generally monogram based, some are difficult to represent in printed orthography as they consist of stippled hand-drawn letters, many surrounded by diamonds, triangles, and stars. In one case, the mark is an arrow going to the left that more resembles a sailor's tattoo than anything orthographical.[11]

In some industries, like timber, monogram- and symbol-based signs proliferated: the marks of the merchant, shipper, quality, port inspector, port of destination, and recipient were inscribed, carved, or branded on the wood. So numerous and confusing were these signs that several handbooks came into being, their pages filled with cryptic hieroglyphs that rather resemble secret or guild-like code.[12] Such in-house codes had long been part of the maritime world, whether for lighthouse signals or semaphores. The complexity of these communication systems increased exponentially with the advent of telegraph code systems, which minimized telegram costs and enabled secrecy.[13] These codes proliferated across a range of domains, whether the police, the railway, or meteorological services. As hubs of communication, ports also relied on secret telegraph codes that were used by merchants and importers dealing in particular commodities (like the "cotton code" referred to in the introduction) as well as dockside authorities, including the Customs service. These different cipher systems, whether marks and numbers or telegraphic code, sedimented in the Custom House, layered onto the feudal insignia inherited from London. The result was a recondite repertoire of codes and protocols that few outsiders could fathom, giving Customs a masonic air, as noted earlier.

In cases where cargo had to be stopped and searched, Customs inspectors had to "read" the cargo itself, rather than just its covering. In such instances, officials were driven to the objects themselves, sniffing, tasting, and feeling the items in front of them in an attempt to classify them or settle disputes about their classification. They minutely checked thread counts in fabric; they opened cartons to verify the weight of items; they tested alcohol to see whether its label matched its content.

A Calcutta Customs manual on how to check the thread count (reckoned in this instance by the area of fabric in relation to its weight) captures this type of labor well while suggesting the ways in which the commodity itself shaped this work. The length part of the equation was fairly straightforward and involved measuring the selvage. Gauging width, however, presented various problems, and Customs officials were enjoined to proceed as follows:

A double-fold of the cloth should be laid on the table and the creases stroked out, so that it may lie perfectly flat. The measuring rod should then be placed across the cloth, and the finger and thumb run down the rod on each side of it across the cloth so as to once more flatten the creases. Care should be taken in doing this to see that whilst the creases are smoothed out, stretching is avoided and the warp threads remain perpendicular to the rod. The measurement should then be recorded.

Officials also had to think about the type of material they were dealing with:

In taking these measurements the peculiarities of the cloth under measure should not be lost sight of. Thus cloths, like grey shirtings, that are pressed but not folded gain slightly, but by no means uniformly, in breadth in the course of pressing; whilst those that are folded, like mulls, lose in the folding more than they gain in the pressing.... Loose cloths like mulls, especially if shrunk in the course of manufacture, are naturally liable to bag and stretch more than others, and owing to their flimsiness it is difficult to apply the first method of measurement satisfactorily; such cloths also are liable to drag in the weaving towards the end of a long piece, and the folds will sometimes not coincide with the weft. Due allowances should be made for these characteristics.[14]

These procedures required that Customs officials apprentice themselves to the objects they worked with, learning the minute peculiarities of the commodities under their jurisdiction. In effect, they functioned as a type of assayer, learning to define and determine composition by touch, feel, and handling. In larger Customs stations, examiners and surveyors could specialize in particular areas, and in big US establishments, officials were recruited from particular industries to capitalize on their dedicated expertise in certain classes of goods. In more modest establishments, jack-of-all-trades officers developed skills of identification and classification across an astonishing array of commodities. Such examiners spent their days among a gallimaufry of objects, from the predictable (sugar, rice, coal) to the obscure (galloons, gimps, and petershams—trimmings used in upholstery and millinery).

In cases where the cargo was suspect, such determinations assumed an epidemiological dimension: Were the goods contaminated, dangerous, adulterated, or seditious? Might a shaving brush contain anthrax? Could a walking stick conceal a dangerous weapon? In smaller ports, Customs officials relied on sight, smell, and touch to diagnose such cases, but in bigger ports, specialists like the plant or animal inspector took over this role. As we shall see in chapter 4, the Customs censor was in part modeled on such a specialist, a print inspector who treated suspect books rather like an invasive species.[15]

The flip side of this epidemiological hermeneutic was to seek out marks that might exonerate the object. One such inscription was the mark of origin ("made in England," etc.), which I discuss in some detail since it played a role in shaping understandings of copyright. The requirements for this mark arose from the empire-wide Merchandise Marks Act of 1887 (promulgated first in 1862, the law did not mention Britain's colonies and dependencies, an oversight corrected in 1887). This legislation specified that all commodities passing through Customs bear a mark indicating where they had been made. Such a mark could only be a fiction, but it was firmly insisted on to enable the implementation of preferential Customs agreements, antidumping provisions, the collection of statistics, and protection against imports from "suspect" countries. In an era of free trade, the act instituted a weak form of protectionism, requiring foreign goods to declare themselves in a British market by carrying a mark of origin. In the wider empire, the act was an attempt to safeguard British goods against imitations.[16]

The provisions of this act were as byzantine as they were extensive, and by the early twentieth century, subcommittees of the Board of Trade in London issued empire-wide instructions and standing orders on the marking of anything from hair combs, to glue and gelatin, to picture and greeting cards, to metal spools for typewriters.[17] Handbooks and manuals likewise advised exporters on how their products were to be marked.[18] The decision on where the mark should appear was in part determined by the object itself: on the stem of the pipe, on the face of the clock, every two yards on the selvage of fabric, on the address section of a postcard, on the rind of the bacon, on the flange of the printing block, and so on. In the case of chilled beef, each side had to bear an indication of origin "in a continuous series of words . . . extending longitudinally: From the hock joint to the neck . . . provided that . . . if the name of the country of production comprises more than one word, such words may be placed vertically one beneath the other instead of in a continuous line."[19] The question of how this information was to be imprinted on the object produced yet further regulations, and the handbooks on the topic are veritable thesauri of inscription replete with instructions on how objects had variously to be impressed, embossed, die-stamped, cast, engraved, etched, printed, applied, stamped, incised, stenciled, painted, branded, molded, punched, or cast, along with an appropriate range of adverbs: *indelibly, visibly, conspicuously, durably*.[20] The choice of inscription method was largely determined by the surface of the commodity itself.

Reading marks of origin was not always straightforward. Was the phrase "A Present from Margate" on a piece of china a mark of origin or not? The answer in this instance was "no" since the phrase was regarded as being intrinsic to the item rather than being inscribed post hoc.[21] Titles of books were likewise regarded as forming part of the commodity itself and hence were not to be treated as a mark of origin. The necessity of spelling this out, as Customs regulations did, indicates that at least some officials might have construed the title as an identifying mark of origin applied to the product itself. Titles like *From Russia, with Love* or *England Made Me* might well have been construed as marks of origin.

A further dimension of Customs scrutiny pertained to the language and script in which the mark of origin was to be inscribed. Any script could be used as long as roman lettering was also present. Any language could be used, but in the British Empire, English generally had to appear as well. Yet, in following this injunction, importers had to be careful since language itself could legally be construed as a mark of origin. As one handbook explained, "If any names, trade-marks, or descriptions in the English language or any English words at all appear on the goods, wrappings or containers, they are considered. . . . as purporting to be of British origin." Goods produced outside Britain but with English markings had to carry clear signs of what was called *counterindication* showing that despite the English words on the product, the commodity had not been manufactured in Britain. Exporters from the United States were advised that "the words 'Made in the U.S.A.' in letters as large and as conspicuous as any other English wording, should be printed on every article, label, or wrapper bearing any words in the English language." In some cases, the mania for inscription went to extraordinary lengths. In the case of writing paper, "if so much as a watermark containing English lettering appears in sheets of paper, a counter-indication of origin must also be watermarked into each sheet, wherever the water-mark occurs."[22]

These dockside economies of attention produced an intimacy between official and object. In response to a query about the status of poppy seed for use by bakers, a collector of customs sent the following almost-loving account of a fancy bread: "The seed is not only used for garnishing bread and cakes but a bread cake, a sample of which I send under separate cover, made by the importers of the seed, which has, in addition to garnishing, a small quantity—about a teaspoonful—a sweetening mixture added, in the center of the article of food."[23]

Customs officials became expert at "women's" knowledge: they were familiar with styles of interior decoration; they knew how fancy breads and confectionery were made; they could describe women's clothing with precision ("silk-lined tea-gown," "lace-finished day-dress"); they knew which type of material was used for underskirts and that gingham was used for cheap dresses (although they were flummoxed by exactly what constituted a "lady's trimmed hat"—was it a ready-to-wear hat or a girl's school hat?—and by slippers that were annoyingly genderless).[24]

The examiners' intimate knowledge of commodities encompassed a quasi-biographical appreciation of the object's trajectory from its origin to its destination. With regard to cloth, examiners were aware of the market for which it was headed and how it might change once there. In southern Africa any surveyor would have known that German and Italian prints and sateens, once imported, changed their guise and entered the market as loincloths for the "native trade."[25] Item 47 of the South African tariff was entitled "Shawling," defined as "wraps for covering the back and shoulders," more specifically "cotton scarves, handkerchiefs and mats exceeding in size 1,600 square inches, that is 40 inches square or its equivalent whether imported singly or joined together by a fringe or weft."[26] Most officers, however, were aware that once in the market, such shawling transmogrified into "kidungas, cadungas, Zanzibar shawls, ... Congo Mats and [was] sometimes invoiced as Printed Calicos, Gordon Tartans, Animal Pattern Calicoes."[27] In one instance, an examiner rejected a consignment of flannelette under item 47 since the fabric was generally used for cheap underskirts and hence could not be classified as shawling.[28] A conflict about whether a white honeycomb bed covering was a quilt or a blanket was settled by an official who decreed the item a quilt since it was used as such "by every European family" in Johannesburg.[29]

The intimacy of examiner and commodity demonstrates the patient provocation that objects exerted over many years. Objects elicited an ongoing "conversation of gestures" as inspectors were required to taste, measure, sniff, and sample objects that crossed the dockside. In these interactions objects were aided by the marine environment itself, which helped shape the rhythm and location of such gestures. As this chapter has demonstrated, the hydrocolonial hermeneutic of the dockside was wrought in this three-way interaction of official, object, and environment.

3

Copyright on a Hydrocolonial Frontier

Most nineteenth-century sea travelers would have been familiar with the phrase "the Chops of the Channel." The term referred to the jaws, or chops, of the English Channel and hence to its entrance, signaled to the north by Land's End and the Isles of Scilly. This stretch of sea was fabled—the setting of early skirmishes against the Spanish Armada in 1588 and, for ocean-weary English sailors, a herald of home.

To ships' passengers, the Chops signaled yet something else, namely, that it was time to sort through their books in preparation for encountering Customs officials in port. As an 1849 passengers' manual explained, these officers paid particular attention to copyright, especially pirated US editions of English authors. These reprints "can endure no longer than the voyage" (as the manual phrased it), and many such volumes must have been tossed into the Chops, to sink slowly into the nether reaches of Davy Jones's library.¹

Yet disposing of volumes overboard did not end the preparations that book-burdened voyagers had to make. As the manual gratuitously reminded its readers, books are "cumbrous appendages to the traveller." Like friends, they could improve on greater acquaintance but could equally cause "inconvenience or disappointment." And inconvenient these textual companions certainly proved to be. Passengers had to sort their books by place and date of publication as well as by language. In terms of place, travelers had to distinguish those volumes printed in British possessions from those originally produced in Britain but exported elsewhere. Books produced outside the British Empire constituted yet another pile. Bookish passengers also had to keep an eye on the date of publication, sorting their volumes into those that appeared before and after 1801. This year marked the Act of Union between Great Britain and Ireland, the latter being a long-standing center of reprinting so that the copyright status of books printed there before and after 1801 differed.² Each of these various categories attracted a different duty reckoned by imperial hundredweight (112 pounds). Maps and drawings were levied with a tax of one penny each, and pictures and paintings at one shilling per square foot.³

As the bewildered passengers disembarked, one might anticipate that the Customs officials would have a better grasp of the situation. In most cases pertaining to copyright, however, the examiners from the Custom House were as baffled as the passengers. These officials faced a snarl of conflicting legislation spread across copyright, Customs administration, and the Merchandise Marks Act. It was difficult to know which law applied where, and as Lionel Bently and others have noted, the British Empire teemed with an "extraordinary multiplicity" of copyright legislation.⁴

How did Customs examiners deal with this farrago? This chapter explores this question, first setting out the byzantine layers of confusion that existed around copyright and then examining how Customs officials solved these problems. After explaining the practical and legal intricacies of the situation, we return to epidemiological themes of the hydrocolonial frontier, showing how British copyright came to be construed as a cipher of propriety, a sign that the volume had been manufactured in Britain and hence was implicitly "white" and respectable. The chapter then traces how copyright unfolded beyond the dockside among merchants, the state, settlers, and African intellectuals and in conclusion asks what these practices of copyright contribute to historiographies on the topic.

IN DURBAN IN 1915, Customs inspectors seized a consignment of foreign reprints that included copies of *Treasure Island* and *Kidnapped*. The collector of customs dithered: should he seize the books in terms of the colonial copyright legislation or the imperial law? While the books languished in the dockside warehouse, this query was batted between Customs and Excise and the Justice Department with no clear answer emerging.[5]

Given the tangle of imperial, colonial, and international copyright law, this level of confusion was not unusual. Imperial law emanated from the metropolis, prioritized the defense of British rights holders, and promoted British publishing in the international arena. The second level—colonial copyright—covered material produced in the colony itself and was generally introduced into settler colonies from the 1850s. The third—international copyright law—was inaugurated by the Berne Convention of 1886 and largely reflected the interests of major European exporters of copyrighted material.[6]

Compounding this jumble was the changing status of foreign (and particularly US) reprints in the empire. The Copyright Amendment Act of 1842 initially prohibited import of such protected works into both Britain and "every part of the British Dominions."[7] The primary focus of this legislation was Canada and the West Indies, both within easy reach of cheap US reprints. The 1842 act sought to prevent the circulation of US publications but in so doing pushed up the price of books in these regions since these had to be imported from England. After strenuous Canadian lobbying, the law was changed with a new 1847 copyright act, known as the Foreign Reprints Act. British possessions (or at least those who signed up for the system) could legally import pirated editions of British copyright work provided a duty of between 10 and 15 percent was paid by the importer—the duty in theory (but seldom in practice) being remitted back to the publisher in Britain. The Australian colonies, great consumers of US reprints, pointedly remained outside the system. Except for Canada, returns from the various colonies were virtually nonexistent. Driven by the ubiquity of cheap US reprints and the inability of the British publishing industry, at least initially, to meet the needs of these markets, the 1847 act remained in place until 1911. The system has been characterized as farcical, both then and now.[8]

As an aside, it is worth noting the role that cheap American reprints played in shaping ideas of print and copyright in the British Empire. By providing a steady stream of books for both a domestic and an international market, the US reprint trade offered a model for what the book as an educational instrument should be—cheap and accessible. In a context where printed books represented a form of soft imperial power, the US model was often invoked by imperial enthusiasts. Speaking to the Royal Commission on Copyright in 1878, Charles Trevelyan advocated the reprinting of English copyright works in India (and elsewhere) as a means of "civilizing" the exponentially expanding number of readers.[9]

The system enabled by the Foreign Reprints Act of 1847 not only created considerable confusion but also generated a lumbering bureaucracy. Forms listing British copyright works were sent from London on a three-monthly basis to every Customs post in those parts of the empire that signed up for the system.[10] These documents were meant to be filed and then consulted, page by laborious page, to discover whether a work was legitimate or not. The maddening complexity of these lists is perhaps best captured in a return from a Customs official in Durban who listed the novel *The Mill on the Floss* with Oliver Cromwell as its author.[11] In most cases, officials avoided the forms, leaving thousands of pages to accumulate in entirely unused loose-leaf files, slowly moldering in the humid atmosphere of the foreshore.

A further area of confusion arose from Customs law itself and the way its provisions related to those of copyright legislation. A letter from the South African commissioner of customs and excise in 1957 captures this point well. As new copyright legislation was in the pipeline, the registrar of copyright had written to the commissioner asking for his input on the section pertaining to Customs and its powers to seize pirated material. The commissioner wrote back indicating that all seizures were done under Customs, not copyright law, and that "not a single instance can be traced where this Department found it necessary to invoke [the copyright law]."[12] The commissioner rather blithely suggested that the section on Customs' power to seize could be dropped from the new copyright bill. The commissioner's assessment was of course wrong; the archive shows that there were indeed cases of seizure under copyright legislation. However, from the redoubt of the head office, the commissioner felt that Customs law and its accompanying regulations were all that was needed to deal with copyright.

This proprietary attitude toward the administration of copyright constituted a long-standing theme in the history of Customs and Excise. In 1918 the South African *Government Gazette* included a notice of regulations pertaining to a new Patents, Designs, Trade Marks and Copyright Act of 1916. The regulations had been drawn up by the collector of customs. The registrar of copyright sent a rather bemused letter indicating that he had not been consulted and asking that in future his views be taken into account.[13]

Another piece of legislation compounding the confusion was the 1887 Merchandise Marks Act (details set out in the previous chapter). In addition to requiring a mark of origin, the act, also known as the Criminal Law of False Marking, aimed to curb false trade descriptions: forged trademarks; misleading indications of weight, quantity, composition, and the like; and contravention of "patent, privilege and copyright." The legislation complicated the job description of Customs examiners and created conflicting ideas about what constituted authority and initiative at different levels in any Custom House. The law extended the number of prohibitable goods and so, in theory at least, required officers to devote more time to the task than they had done previously or, in official parlance, "than is ordinarily bestowed [for examination] for revenue purposes."[14] Yet the decisions to be made about false trade descriptions were abstruse and ambiguous; as a handbook commented, "A very difficult and delicate task is thus thrown upon the officers of Customs." "It is quite evident," the handbook continues, "that in many cases the officers of Customs, who are not experts, could not possibly, from their knowledge, judge between a trade description and a false trade description."[15] The Indian *Merchandise Marks Manual* was more to the point: "The occasions on which Customs Officers should take action on their own initiative will naturally be rare."[16]

The initiative instead shifted outside the Customs House, to booksellers and publishers who could tip off the collector about their competitors whom they suspected of bringing in pirated material. Once alerted, Customs could seize the consignment, a process known as "detention on information." In legal parlance, the act gave "the persons who are specially interested in the goods, liberty to secure their detention by the Crown officers, provided that those who claim their interferences should give security to protect the Crown from any action for damages for what might afterwards turn out to be a wrongful detention."[17] The security was meant to deter false accusations, but it did not always do so, and in some cases publishers and booksellers used the mechanism to stall the consignments of their competitors.

On the ground, then, it was unclear what powers ordinary officers possessed. In the course of "ordinary examination for revenue purposes," could they detain falsely marked goods "without previous information," or should they proceed only in the case of "information by an informant"?[18] In some cases, during the course of "ordinary examination," officers could not help but stumble across copyright infringements. One such case arose in 1930 in Windhoek in what is now Namibia, then South-West Africa (a German colony placed under South African mandate after 1918). A Customs examiner discovered sixty copies of *Lady Windermere's Fan*, part of the Tauchnitz series printed in Leipzig. The front cover conspicuously announced that it was not to be introduced into Great Britain or her colonies. Assuming that it was a clear-cut case, the officer detained the consignment, only to learn subsequently that the books had to be released as imperial copyright legislation did not apply in mandated states, or so at least the attorney general thought.[19]

In 1906 in Cape Town, three cases of books from the SS *Susquehanna*, which had sailed from New York, were detained. Eighty-three of these books were "of American origin" from the Mershon Company, a firm that specialized in reprinting juvenile fiction and classics. The suspect volumes included works by John Ruskin and Robert Browning and popular novels like *Lorna Doone* and *Black Beauty*. Working from the three-monthly lists of British copyright work sent from London, the collector of customs deemed these books to be reprints of British copyright work and planned to detain them. He was, however, overridden by the attorney general, who held that Customs had to produce evidence that the books had been copyrighted in Britain "either by oral evidence or by means of certified copy, under the hand of the officer appointed by the Stationers' Company."[20]

Importers and booksellers added to the confusion by introducing their own interpretations of the law. In 1906 a translation series entitled Universal-Bibliothek, produced in Leipzig and imported into the Cape Colony, fell foul of Customs and Excise: a letter of appeal argued that under the Berne Convention, the series was entirely legitimate.[21] Some merchants attempted to tutor Customs inspectors on how to detect pirated reprints while alerting them to the possibility of illegal imports. The importer of *Bentley's Complete Phrase Code Book* urged officials to watch out for cheap imitations of his product. The telltale signs would be inferior binding, indistinct printing, and the absence of the publisher's London address from the title page.[22] An agent of *Encyclopaedia Britannica* asked Customs officials to be on the lookout for US reprints: an indicative sign would be the absence of the Edinburgh printer's name, R & R Clark.[23]

Canny merchants used the confusion of Customs to their own advantage. Thomas Maskew Miller, a bookseller and publisher in Cape Town who specialized in the textbook market, ran rings around Customs, using their own regulations against them. In 1917 a new copyright law had been passed, and Customs was required to publish regulations to accompany the legislation. This task was duly performed, but the regulations only mentioned how copyright registration was to occur, with no indication of the procedures to be followed by Customs in the case of copyright disputes. Spotting this oversight, Miller took full advantage. He claimed (quite brazenly and incorrectly) that he held copyright on a consignment of a Dutch novel, *Piet Uys*, brought in by one of his competitors, J. H. De Bussy. The collector asked him for proof of his proprietorship. Miller quickly requested via his lawyers the regulations pertaining to disputed copyright, knowing full well that these did not yet exist.[24] At this point the correspondence ceases, so the final outcome is not known. However, evidence elsewhere shows Miller to have been a dogged and litigious businessman who used the intricacies of law and legal proceedings (both real and threatened) to cow and exhaust his competitors.[25]

If one moved beyond the Custom House, matters did not improve. Senior colonial officials were, if anything, even less informed about copyright than Customs personnel. In 1896 the colony of Natal passed copyright legislation intended to provide for the registration of publications produced in the colony. The attorney general had only the vaguest idea of what was involved in copyright and in drafting the legislation did not specify two critical details: the place of first publication and the nationality of the author. As a legal commentator notes, the legislation meant that "publication anywhere in the world of the works of authors of whatever nationality created copyright in Natal."[26] The Colonial Office in London was aghast and dispatched a finger-wagging letter, noting that while several clauses of the Natal law "are for the most part copied from the Imperial Acts they have, from insufficient acquaintance with the reasons which govern the peculiar provisions of those Acts, become confused, tautological and contradictory."[27] One cannot help having some sympathy for the Natal attorney general. Was there anyone, anywhere, who grasped the "peculiar provisions" of copyright legislation in the British Empire?

IN DEALING WITH THIS confusion, Customs examiners hewed to their own practices. In legal terms, they leaned toward the Merchandise Marks Act and ignored copyright legislation where they could. In this approach they were supported by the Justice Department, which advised the collector of customs to deal with "alleged infringement of South African Copyright works as in the case of infringements of Merchandise Marks Act."[28] The publishing and printing industry also favored this act as the preferred instrument against copyright infringements and lobbied for a local version of the law to defend South African books against reprinting (in 1926 Afrikaans children's books had been reprinted in Japan).[29]

This reliance on the Merchandise Marks Act was understandable since it dovetailed with the concerns of Customs officials, namely, how to manage trade goods in transit and what kinds of marks they needed to cross boundaries. The act focused closely on the marking that goods required and the way one might diagnose cases of counterfeiting and false marking—in short, exactly the preoccupations of the Custom House. The logic of the mark ran deep in the Custom House: Customs officials were expert readers of various inscriptions—whether marks and numbers, trademarks, or marks of origin—which they understood as externally imposed. This logic is apparent in the practice of requiring false trademarks or obscene images to be removed from cargo before it could proceed on its way (as noted earlier, a task that only white labor could perform).[30] Another indication arises from a form to be filled out by merchants seeking detention of suspect books, where applicants were asked to identify "initials or marks (if any) usually placed on copies of work."[31] It is difficult to imagine what such a mark might be, but in the thinking of Customs officials, the book should behave like other pieces of cargo and carry its own marks and numbers.

The Merchandise Marks Act itself accorded books even less special treatment where they fell under the category of goods, namely, anything that was the subject of "trade, manufacture, or merchandise." Under earlier copyright legislation in Britain, books had enjoyed a special status and were considered distinct from mere goods. However, under the Merchandise Marks Act, books were downgraded into the larger category of trade objects. The act concerned itself with trade markings, trade descriptions, marks of origin, and "patent, privilege and copyright," an environment in which copyright became a matter of trade description and place of origin, akin to the trademark. If false, copyright constituted a false trade description; if true, it could be taken to be an "indirect indication of British manufacture."[32]

Copyright was but one mark in a galaxy of inscriptions circulating on the dockside. As the South African regulations indicated, these concerned "number, quantity, measure, or weight of any goods; the place or country in which goods were produced; the mode of manufacture or production of the goods; the material of which any goods are composed; any goods being subject to an existing patent, privilege, or copyright or the use of any figure, word, or mark which according to the custom of the trade is commonly taken to be an indication of any of these."[33]

Copyright was overshadowed by, or subsumed under, the trademark and mark of origin. The elaborate instructions for how to inscribe a mark of origin in a book demonstrate the preeminence that Customs attached to this sign as opposed to copyright, which by comparison shrinks in significance. For the Canadian market, the mark of origin had to be inscribed in one of the following ways: "by printing or die-stamping indelibly or by blind embossing or die-stamping (if legible); on inside or outside of front or back cover, the first or last page or the title pages, 'Printed (or lithographed) in——— (name of country, or name of city, state, or other division of country).'"[34]

WHILE THE MERCHANDISE MARKS ACT assigned copyright a lesser symbolic role on the dockside, the instrument was not entirely idle. Deployed on a hydro-colonial border, copyright could be enlisted for other purposes. Take, for instance, a file entitled "Prohibitions" kept in the small port of Knysna in the Cape. Running from 1910 to 1936, the file preserves the memos from the head office on what the Knysna Customs officials should be on the lookout for. Alongside pirated photographs that violated copyright, examiners had to keep their eyes skinned for copies of the banned film of the 1910 boxing match between Jack Johnson and James Jeffries, in which the African American Johnson knocked out his white American opponent. Other items included indecent postcards; a banned novel about the Anglo-Boer War, entitled *The Transvaal Surrounded*; shaving brushes with a "virulent infection" of anthrax; noxious weeds; watches with fake sovereigns attached; handkerchiefs embroidered with obscene images for the "native market"; Radcliffe Hall's *Well of Loneliness*; butter from an area infected with foot-and-mouth disease; "communistic" pamphlets; and live parrots.[35]

In such files, the category "Prohibition" runs together a toxic mix of obscenity, sedition, racial insubordination, piracy, and pathogens. While copyright has little power against this brew, it stands as a miniature and symbolic bulwark, a sign that a copyrighted book had been manufactured in Britain and so enjoyed a probity and integrity that the other objects did not. In this context, copyright becomes a type of eugenic trademark, a sign of an implicit racial virtue in contrast to the implied racial decline promised by the Johnson-Jeffries film. Hall's novel would of course have been copyrighted and manufactured in Britain and so seems to cut across this argument. However, Customs may well have followed the logic, long established in British courts, that obscene, libelous, immoral, or seditious works were not protected by copyright.[36] From this perspective, copyright functions as a sign of probity and propriety, refusing to accredit a harmful object and hence to permit it to enter the market, as though the copyright itself were a Customs officer.

This logic of the mark of origin resonated with other dockside regimes, most notably the immigration-restriction procedures of excluding those with the wrong bodily mark of origin and using the notorious writing and dictation test, by means of which would-be immigrants, as a condition of entry, could be required to write a dictated passage in a European language and in roman script. Books with British copyright carried a reassuring mark of origin, a type of racial trademark that lifted them above suspicion. With regard to trademarks proper, such racialization was routine and explicit. White labor unions ensured that trademarks on the goods they produced reflected the racial "origin" of the product. In California in the 1870s, the inscription "White Men's Labor Cigars" signaled that the merchandise had not been made by Chinese migrant labor and that the buyer was hence saved from inhaling the racial contamination that white workers imagined such labor might occasion.[37]

This racialization was inscribed in the institution of copyright itself. Across European empires (and in their metropolises), copyright was presumptively white. German imperial copyright law, for example, prohibited *Eingeborene* ("natives") from holding copyright.[38] While British copyright law in the dominions did not specify categories of persons, its imagined subject appeared to be white men (white women could hold copyright but had to indicate their marital status since this impacted on whether they could hold property). In South Africa, whenever Native Affairs Department officials discussed copyright, they debated whether their own internal publications should be registered under the provisions of the law or not. That their "native subjects" might be affected by or wish to partake of such legislation never occurred to them—in their mind, it was a white man's right.[39] These assumptions had indeed been inherent in copyright legislation all along: to hold copyright, one had to be a free, sovereign, rights- and property-holding individual, a category that until 1834 presupposed racialized slavery as its condition of possibility.[40]

IN TRACING COPYRIGHT beyond the port, one important factor to bear in mind is the size and shape of the colonial southern African printing and publishing industry, which was a small and uncertain undertaking. Book markets were limited, and distribution was difficult, making "the right to control distribution by limiting copying . . . a right of precarious value," as Meredith Mc-

Gill argues for the nineteenth-century United States.[41] In this context, copyright, like any legal instrument, was shaped and reshaped by the contexts into which it traveled.[42] Fashioned on the dockside by logistic and boundary-making imperatives, the Customs views of copyright penetrated into three domains: the merchant elite, the state, and settler society. A fourth group, African writers, elaborated a different view of copyright that became a method of claiming rights and constituting themselves as rights-bearing subjects.

As we have seen, merchants deployed copyright not as a matter of authorial property but more as a business strategy to outwit their competitors. This approach had been inherited from Customs regulations and the Merchandise Marks Act, which encouraged merchants to tell on each other's supposed copyright violations. As in the Australian case, copyright functioned as a minor instrument by which merchant elites competed with each other while attempting to consolidate their economic position.[43]

The state itself had little interest in copyright, as is apparent from the ongoing confusion about which department should best oversee it—Treasury, Education, the Interior?[44] When the state was required to engage more closely with copyright, it adopted the epidemiological hermeneutic of Customs. Such an occasion arose in 1961 in the wake of South Africa leaving the British Commonwealth and becoming a republic. In that year, the prime minister's office had asked all departments what part they could play in defending the new national symbols, like the flag, coat of arms, and national anthem. The question of the national anthem was especially pertinent, since in a climate of growing Afrikaner nationalism, a new anthem, "Die Stem van Suid-Afrika" (The voice of South Africa), had recently been introduced to trump "God Save the Queen." In a large and lavish ceremony, the copyright for this new anthem had been ceded to the South African state.[45]

In response to the prime minister's request, the collector of customs and excise indicated that his department was prepared to defend the republic against illegal copies of the anthem that might enter the country from outside, which would immediately be confiscated. Who, one wonders, in 1961 might have wanted to flood South Africa with counterfeit copies of its own national anthem, in any event largely sung in Afrikaans, an official English translation notwithstanding? The Russians? Who might have cunningly made pirated Afrikaans gramophone records, possibly with embedded propaganda messages? The British? Who in a fit of pique might have produced spoof versions of the national anthem in retaliation for South Africa deserting the Commonwealth? While entirely Monty Pythonesque, this story points to the tenaciousness of an epidemiological hermeneutic in which copyright was imagined as a border-control mechanism, keeping contaminated material out of the body politic.

For settler society, copyright functioned as a way of validating colonial knowledge. The number of items copyrighted was small (in the 1890s, about ninety a year in the Cape Colony, about two dozen a year in the Transvaal, and one dozen a year in Natal).[46] A large proportion of the items copyrighted were classic genres of colonial epistemology: maps; grammars and dictionaries of indigenous languages; manuals on agriculture, hunting, and botany; handbooks on dealing with servants. Indeed, so negligible was the work of this office that when the state had any queries on copyright, these were referred to Customs and Excise. If the copyright registry office had any value, it probably lay in a symbolic demonstration of statecraft and the exercise of copyright as a display of white authority.

This settler use of copyright can also be construed as part of a larger discourse field, namely, the notion that settlers believed they had a copyright on civilization. Drawing implicitly on ideas of whiteness as property, settlers alternatively belittled and attacked those who illegitimately "copied" "European" forms. As the postcolonial debates on mimicry have indicated, this idea of copying was experienced as an existential assault and, one might add, an affront to ideas of property holding. The vicious energy with which white workingmen sought to maintain printing as a white industry speaks to the same themes as does the endlessly retailed idea that writing itself was European.[47] Only settlers had the right to copy and to the means of copying.

One group who were keen users of copyright were African writers. Like embattled groups elsewhere, they regarded copyright as a strategy to claim a right, however limited, and to constitute oneself as a credentialed subject.[48] Book bearing might be translated into rights bearing (an act that ironically reflected on and balanced out other forms of forced book bearing, like passes). In deploying copyright in this way, African writers adopted a portfolio approach to authorship, adding a further option to an existing repertoire of forms of cultural authority derived from traditional intellectual resources, from Christianity, and from their status as an educated elite.[49] These strategies are apparent from the title page of a collection of isiXhosa praise poems entitled *Zemk'inkomo magwalandini* ("There go your cattle, you cowards!" or "The cattle are being driven off by the enemy, you cowards!," a Xhosa war cry and call to arms. The term can also be construed more generally as "Defend your heritage").[50] The author is W. B. Rubusana (1858–1936), a prominent member of South Africa's Black elite. On the title page, his name is followed by a miniature curriculum vitae: he has a PhD, is "the first black member of Parliament in South Africa" (he was a member of the Cape Provincial Council), is a minister of the Presbyterian Church, and is president of the South African Native Convention. Rubusana's other books are listed: *Steps to Christ* (a translation), the *Presbyterian Service Book, Jesus Is Coming,* and so on. The lower half of the page tells us that the book has been entered at Stationers' Hall in London and that it is the second edition printed for the author by the company Burton and Tanner, operating in Frome (Somerset) and London.

Rubusana could well have produced the book in the Cape Colony, but there would have been various drawbacks; most notably, it would have been subject to the strictures and condescension of the white-controlled Christian mission press, the only printers permitted to composite material in African languages (a ploy by white printers to keep cheaper African compositors out of their domain).[51] With regard to copyright, Rubusana would have had to register his book in the Deeds Office in Cape Town, which would technically have secured protection of his rights across the British Empire. Instead, he chose to produce the book and register its copyright in Britain. The market for the book lay in South Africa, but Rubusana nonetheless wanted it to bear the imprimatur of the imperial capital, both in its production and in its claiming of the highest copyright authority.

Black writers like Rubusana deployed copyright as a means to claim rights. Settler society, merchants, and the colonial state, by contrast, turned copyright into yet a further instrument of racial supremacy. This dispensation is almost the opposite of what contemporary debates on intellectual property lead us to believe. These generally hold that the so-called developing world ignores intellectual property because of its communal or "traditional" orientations, as opposed to the individualism of Western property law. The southern African picture inverts this: African writers defended copyright, while the settler representatives of the West turned copyright into a racialized practice.

CAN THESE TRAJECTORIES of colonial copyright add anything to the substantial body of work on Euro-American copyright? As this scholarship indicates, copyright law has long done the cultural labor of configuring personhood and property, which have been wrought via a raft of legal fictions: the author as genius, originality, literary property. The rich legacy of work on copyright has deftly unpicked these fictions, which has given this scholarship a strong author-centric orientation.[52] The view from the dockside provides a different perspective. Customs officials had little interest in the author of a book, focusing much more on its manufacture and origin. Given the dockside confusion around what copyright meant, the idea of authors' rights gained little traction. A further factor demoting the author was the definition of the book as a minor category of paper and stationery. Beyond the port, copyright mutated yet further, becoming a technique to consolidate merchant advantage, a vector of the epidemiological imagination, a minor instrument of settler statecraft, a technique of whiteness, and a method to claim rights.

These dockside views of copyright take us back to earlier instantiations of copyright practice. Indeed, examining the Custom House protocols around copyright is rather like stepping back into Stationers' Hall in London in the seventeenth and eighteenth centuries. As Adrian Johns indicates, the Stationers' Company construed copyright as a form of property and propriety that signaled the good standing of the copyholder.[53] The examiners in the colonial Customs House attached ideas of propriety to copyright but with a different inflection. Here copyright conferred propriety on the object itself, a sign that it was an upright product of British manufacture and could be granted entry.

As this chapter has demonstrated, these logics of copyright were produced by the colonial maritime frontier and its hydrocolonial imperatives. The dockside provides a surprisingly rich vantage point from which to track alternative histories of copyright.

4

Censorship on a Hydrocolonial Frontier

Having thus far tarried on southern African docksides, let us move briefly to Sydney, where the White Australia policy went hand in hand with zealous maritime boundary making, immigration restriction, and censorship. Here two young men, Dick Searle and John Hall, joined the Sydney Customs service, anticipating an exhilarating career chasing smugglers and dashing about on boats in the harbor. The reality was less glamorous—they ended up in cramped offices scrutinizing printed matter for traces of indecency, obscenity, or blasphemy. After an initial frisson, this work palled as day after day they plodded through piles of publications. As indicated by Deana Heath, who interviewed Searle and Hall, Australian Customs played a central role in creating and sustaining the quarantined culture of border making. Searle's and Hall's censoring efforts contributed to this carceral culture and its attempts to keep out anything that might compromise the moral health of white Australia.[1]

Like Herman Melville's landsmen who harbor "ocean reveries" while "tied to counters, nailed to benches, clinched to desks," Hall and Searle no doubt resented the office-bound labor of the censor.[2] Others took to the task with alacrity. One such enthusiast was Ivo Hammett, the literary examining officer of the Melbourne Custom House. A 1954 newspaper article, "Tasters in Chief—the Customs Story," described his daily routine. His table, we learn, was "piled high with the day's intake—dozens of crime and sex magazines, German sunbathers, English horror stories, *Forever Amber* in German, *Love Me Sailor* in French." The piece continues, "Every book is not read right through—that would be physically impossible."

> "We work it this way," said Mr. Hammett picking up a magazine from his desk. It was a private eye story, full of boots in the face, bullets in the belly, and girls on the couch.
>
> "I flip through it first, just like this. I see the publisher's name—well known for this type of book—see a few objectionable paragraphs and decide if it's suspect."
>
> "Then I go through it more thoroughly, noting the pages giving the greatest offence."[3]

It could well have been someone like Hammett whom Nadine Gordimer had in mind when she observed in 1973 that censors treated literature like a bar of soap (as we noted in the introduction).[4] Having suffered under South African censorship, Gordimer was aware of the history of the institution and its origins in Customs. Indeed, she recalled a famous 1936 case of Customs censorship involving Stuart Cloete's novel *Turning Wheels*, about the Great Trek (the founding myth of Afrikaner nationalism involving the movement of Dutch Boers into the interior of the country in response to the abolition of slavery at the Cape). The books "showed the trekkers as flawed human beings, not entirely shining heroes. They were also explicitly depicted making love—not married love, either. There was lust in the laager. So you can imagine the outcry. I was twelve years old at the time and I remember being very eager somehow to get hold of this wicked, sexy book that was forbidden even to grownups."[5]

Gordimer was neither the first nor the last to portray censors as ignorant. Rehearsing a well-known discourse, she pitted the creative force of imaginative literature against the destructiveness of banning and prohibition.[6] This stark opposition has long been critiqued by a range of scholars of censorship working across regions and periods, who demonstrate that far from being opponents, literature and censorship are entangled in mutual definition (for example, where obscene texts are exempt from censorship on grounds of being high literature).[7] These studies complicate any view of censors as ham-handed buffoons; instead, the current tendency is to portray them as skilled intellectuals and trained literary readers. The takeaway message is clear: censors are more sophisticated than we think.

Yet where does a figure like Hammett fit in? Or indeed the unnamed Australian official who complained that the content of secondhand magazines constituted such a potent contaminant that even the bleaching agent used as a disinfectant in the paper was overcome? Do we simply write this off as an ontological faux pas and return to the figure of the ignorant censor? Can we learn anything from those who tried to read a book as a bar of soap?

This chapter argues that we can. The logic of Customs' reading, shaped by its daily protocols and the exigencies of the port, opens new vistas on ideas of censorship. Across the board (whether portraying censors as ignorant or sophisticated), the scholarship operates from the assumption that censors read what was in front of them. Very often they did, and in great detail. Yet such studies tend to look fairly high up the bureaucratic chain, at specialist committees.[8] This story of the Custom House takes us lower down the chain to figures like Hall and Searle, where censors paid less attention to words than to the object as a whole. What implications does such an object-oriented mode of reading have for notions of censorship and definitions of literature? In exploring these questions, this chapter focuses on two moments: the first is the South African War (Anglo-Boer War) of 1899–1902, when Customs assumed a quasi-military role in censoring and banning pro-Boer material. The second involves the 1920s and 1930s, a period of mounting anticommunism during which Customs officials continued and extended their role as censors. The military censors reinforced the logistic "reading" habits of Customs, while the anticommunism repurposed its epidemiological hermeneutic for ideological ends. This formation laid the groundwork for subsequent censorship regimes in South Africa, which drew on these protocols while also attempting to present the censors as professional readers in contrast to the rank amateurs of the Custom House. This chapter draws out these trajectories, demonstrating the new angles that a fuller focus on the Custom House brings to histories of censorship in South Africa.

IN MARCH 1904 Hjalmar Reitz wrote to the attorney general of the Cape Colony inquiring about fifty copies of his novel that had been seized by Customs authorities. The novel was entitled *De dochter van den handsopper* (The daughter of the hands-upper [a term for Boer fighters who surrendered and joined the British]) and was pro-Boer in its sentiments. Reitz was confused by the detention of his books. The war had ended two years earlier, and as Reitz wrote, he was not aware "that press censorship was still in existence" and asked to whom he should appeal to have the books released.[9] Others were similarly puzzled about the postwar censorship situation. A few weeks earlier, Customs examiners had seized a consignment of pro-Boer books imported from the Netherlands on grounds that "they had to pass the Censor's office." Writing on behalf of the importer, Mr. P. Speelman, the consul general of the Netherlands noted, "As far as I know the Censor's work ended with Martial Law in this Colony."[10] Customs officials themselves were uncertain: once martial law had ceased, what law should they apply to seditious imports?[11]

Since the 1870s, the Customs surveyors of the Cape Colony had been legally empowered to seize goods that were indecent or objectionable.[12] These powers of seizure and confiscation were considerably extended during the war. Cape Town was of course geographically distant from the actual fighting, which unfolded in the interior of the subcontinent. However, the city was a key hub in the conflict. Thousands of troops arrived in its port, while refugees from the war collected in the city, which was gripped by imperial fervor. Pro-Boer publications were publicly burned in bonfires, while the premises of newspapers deemed disloyal were wrecked.[13]

In the Cape Colony, martial law was declared only toward the end of hostilities (and then only in some districts). Customs officials nonetheless worked closely with military personnel from the beginning of the war, granting themselves new powers to seize any import that might be construed as aiding the enemy. In March 1902 (some six weeks before the war ended), the Cape Town collector of customs detained a consignment of Dutch books that had been ordered by the city's library. While one might take this as a vote of civic confidence in the volumes, the collector of customs thought otherwise. The books, he decreed, were "calculated to foster sedition while some contain scandalous libels against the British troops now operating in South Africa and also against

His Majesty's Imperial Government. . . . If not intercepted they would have been put into circulation [by the library] . . . with the result that the atrocious libels they contain would have been widely disseminated in contravention of Proclamation 277 of 12th October 1899 [the proclamation of martial law]."[14]

In January 1905, D. G. Barry and M. Borcherds, landing surveyors in the Cape Town Custom House, seized 450 copies of *Vechten en vlugten van Beyers en Kemp* (Advance and retreat of Beyers and Kemp) by J. F. Naude, a military chaplain and secretary to the two Boer generals named in the title. In a report signed "Docks, Cape Town," the two surveyors wrote, "Opening the book at random, we came across the following which is a translation of the two concluding paragraphs on page 265."[15] The first paragraph describes a battle scene between the First Battalion of General Kitchener's Fighting Scouts and a Boer contingent. The Scouts allow their Black auxiliaries to kill two burgers, whose bodies are dumped in a ditch. The second paragraph details how the English soldiers use Boer women and children as a shield against Boer fire. The surveyors felt that the calumny on the British troops and their auxiliaries was so self-evident that it required no comment.

In another instance, in 1904, a consignment of fifteen pro-Boer books was "arrested." The Cape Town collector of customs produced a report to explain why the volumes were undesirable. Resorting to drastic summary, he lists the titles numerically and then states his complaint against each one: "Nos 1 and 2: novels written in usual exaggerated style laudatory of achievements of Boers; 3: Historical [book], the bulk of which is questionable and has a tendency to minimize the courage of the British; 4, 5 and 6: same as 1 and 2." And so it continued. Number 9 was swept aside as "decidedly of an objectionable nature," while number 10 was consigned to the dust heap by the phrase "page 67 is objectionable."[16]

Not all reports were this terse. In the case of Reitz's *De dochter van den handsopper*, the Customs report picks out seven extracts from a novel of some three hundred pages. Each paragraph is preceded by a set of "stage directions" explaining the context in which the quotation appears: "Page 27 ('Oom Piet' has just lost his daughter; his son, who has been at home for a little while, has to go on commando again; the English are approaching. Oom Piet uses the following expression [referring to the English]) 'Thou children of the devil, they will one day have to suffer for all the misery they bring upon us.'"[17] Yet, even if this report is more extensive than the rest, it bears the imprimatur of the military censor, where any text is treated like war reportage from which disparaging portrayals of British forces must be excised. Novels were read as military intelligence.

Long shaped by carceral histories of slavery and then immigration restriction, Customs and Excise claimed the right to seize any publication they considered seditious. Any pro-Boer books became ready targets both during and after the war, ending up as textual prisoners of war, subject to incarceration and censorship that combined the traditional methods of Customs reading (counting, measuring, sampling) with the sensibility of the military censor ever on the lookout for disloyal portrayals of the British forces and anything that might give succor to the enemy.

IN MAY 1933 an organization called the Committee against the Ban on Working Class Literature wrote to the collector of customs, objecting to the confiscation of three hundred copies of a pamphlet entitled "The Struggle of the Bolsheviks for the Social Insurance of the Proletariat." As the secretary of the committee noted, the letter from Customs announcing the embargo recorded the title as "The Struggle of the Bolsheviks for the Social *Insurrection* of the Proletariat" (emphasis added). This error in the title, the secretary wrote, constituted a telling "commentary on the psychology of the officials concerned, and evidence that the pamphlet was banned without investigation of its contents."[18]

While the collector of customs roundly rejected the allegation, the practice of reading by title (or misreading in this case) was common.[19] Invoices accompanying book consignments listed titles, and officials used these to decide whether to detain material and refer it to the Board of Censors.[20] In the case of a consignment of fifty Gujarati books, the titles were translated into English, and on the basis of these, decisions about placing books in detention were made.[21] Book covers provided another avenue for assaying a publication, with the offending jacket being enough to have the object banned or burned.[22] French novels were categorized as undesirable simply for being French or based on their illustrations.[23] This reliance on readily visible markers is apparent from the attention devoted to the amount of print in a publication, which was used to differentiate stationery from books. Were diaries with almanacs in them stationery or books, one officer wanted to know. The answer was stationery since the amount of printing was small compared to that in a book.[24]

In part, these methods of reading were induced by the exponential increase in books entering South Africa and the ever-expanding range of publications that were potentially suspect and hence had to be checked. As one official noted in 1952, "During the past few years there has been a marked increase in the number of importations of cheap paper-covered books with lurid titles and cover illustrations, as well as political (communistic) treaties, pamphlets, brochures, etc."[25]

These "paper-covered books" (a catchall term for popular fiction, comics, dime novels, and magazines) entered South African ports in growing numbers. Targeted by a range of antivice civic organizations as pernicious and corrupting, these publications were routinely seized by Customs in what they termed a "literature purge" that accounted for some four thousand titles being banned between 1940 and 1956.[26] Also on the increase were "red" journals and other seditious material. As racial segregation tightened, increasing amounts of material came under suspicion: book covers showing "colored" men and "white" women; postcards of Seretse Khama, the first president of independent Botswana, and his fiancée, Ruth Williams; any material that showed conflict between "Europeans" and "natives."[27]

In the wake of the misreading of "insurance" as "insurrection," Customs officials were instructed not only to detain but to read periodicals like the *Moscow Daily News*, *October Revolution and the Trade Unions*, *Militant*, *Negro Worker*, and *New Masses*, which as one official noted caused "considerable labour and trouble."[28] It is unlikely that officials actually heeded these instructions; some took their cue from their ultimate boss, the minister of finance. In 1931 he had a meeting with Louis Joffee, who had been charged with importing "red" journals. Joffee urged the minister to read the *Moscow Daily News* to see for himself how innocuous it actually was. "Do you think I have nothing more to do than read these papers?" retorted the minister.[29]

The increased scale of print material making its way through the port had logistic and practical consequences. Cupboards overflowed with embargoed magazines, while Customs clerks argued about how best to manage "lorry loads" of publications.[30] As censorship became more securitized, the range of players involved in its operation expanded, as did the possibility of confusion between them. In addition to Customs, the post office, the Board of Censors, two different ministries (Interior and Finance), the security services, and the ordinary police played some role in censorship. The Native Affairs Department also weighed in from time to time, alerting Customs to "seditious and inflammatory" material that had crossed its horizon.[31]

The complexity of the situation can be gauged from the desperate pleas of book trade association representatives whose merchandise languished for months in dockside warehouses while different bureaucrats discussed its fate. Some booksellers were drawn into voluntarily submitting their material to the Board of Censors before importing it, even though prepublication censorship was never part of the law.[32] British publishers and publishers' associations attempted to intervene. In August 1940 Lawrence and Wishart, the publisher aligned with the Communist Party of Great Britain, dispatched twenty-two titles to the People's Bookshop in Johannesburg. By November only two had arrived; the others were either banned or languished in bureaucratic limbo.[33]

The byzantine bureaucracy involved made the task of dealing with publications ever more time-consuming. As one chief clerk indicated, in the 1930s a consignment of books would have occupied no more than five minutes of an official's time. By the 1950s, the task had become labyrinthine, and the clerk's account of the procedures is worth quoting at some length:

> The Examining Officer is required to confirm that none of these titles appears in any of the lists in his possession of publications which have already been declared, objectionable, doubtful, etc. (Here reference may be made in parenthesis to the time consumed in Head Office in compiling such lists and at the ports in keeping them up to date). Even if none of the titles invoiced has previously been "listed," the Examining Officer may consider that some of the invoiced titles are questionable or, if they are paper-covered novels, that some of the cover illustrations might bear review, and he has therefore to detain the goods and issue a stop-note. In the Searcher's Office further detailed examination is then necessary, and probably several publications, of which the Examining Office has doubts, have to be referred to the Surveyor. Those of which there are reasonable grounds for doubt have then to be extracted for detention, and forms 77/78 have to be prepared. On receipt in Head Office there is further scrutiny, with the likelihood of reference to the Board of Censors for a recommendation to the Minister, whose decision is then conveyed to this office via the Secretary for the Interior. If the decision is adverse our troubles are not yet ended, for we then have to instruct the port to give notice of seizure and when seizure is complete the port has to seek instructions for disposal, which generally takes the form of accumulating a quantity and sale (after mutilation) for repulping purposes.[34]

The question of disposal created yet further labor. Banned publications were variously burned, cast into the sea, pulped, or torn by hand into "small pieces." In one mind-boggling instance, three hundred titles were destroyed by the last method.[35] In cases where books had been the subject of a court case and had been declared legally offensive, they were dispatched to the mint, where the deputy master personally confirmed that the volumes had been "completely destroyed in a furnace."[36] In rare instances, banned books made a getaway: in 1925 two cases of literature from the Comintern were inadvertently put up for auction in Durban.[37] This practice of auctioning books (or selling them at rummage sales or donating them to lighthouse keepers) was intended only for "innocuous" titles that had been abandoned in Customs and never claimed.

Following the logic of quarantine, Customs officials at times kept items in custody with a view to "correcting" them before releasing them into the world in a healthy state. Examiners tore off objectionable magazine covers and destroyed offending book jackets, allowing the remainder of the publication to proceed. Questionable passages or advertisements were blacked out. In Australia, the New South Wales collector of customs boasted of his particular method—a stamp with a rosette pattern that not only obliterated the pernicious text but had a disconcerting effect on the eye.[38] Films condemned by the Board of Censors were sent back to the custody of Customs officials, where they were "reformed," with sections being defaced or excised before they were permitted to limp out of Customs. False trademarks could be scrubbed off a product, which was then allowed to proceed on its way.[39] Similarly, secondhand clothing that arrived in port was fumigated. Up until the 1930s, films or even offending books could be dispatched back whence they came, or, in Customs parlance, "reshipped to the consignor." In a bureaucratic nicety, the duty on such items was refunded since they were not regarded as having been imported.[40] Such was the fate of the film *Battleship Potemkin*, which the Board of Censors deemed "realism carried to excess, gruesome to a degree and . . . clever propaganda" before sending it home in disgrace.[41]

However, as the pitch of anticommunism mounted, offending items were destroyed rather than being deported. When the South African Society for Peace and Friendship attempted to import *Ivan Tavlov*, the film was banned for propagating "undesirable political ideologies" and burned.[42] From the late 1940s, any films headed for the Russian embassy in South Africa fell under suspicion and were seized by Customs, thereby saving the South African public from such uplifting offerings as *Song of Youth*, *A Summer Harvest*, and *A Glorious Jubilee*. In one instance, while detaining a batch of Soviet films, Customs confiscated the ambassador's cinema projector along with his wine and caviar.[43]

Given the time-consuming labor of detaining, seizing, processing, transporting, and mutilating or destroying undesirable publications, the chief clerk noted, "May I suggest that the time is opportune to indicate that customs officers are not protectors of the public morals and that, having regard to shortage of staff in general and trained customs officers in particular, it would be desirable to relieve the department of much of the censorship of literature involved?" The clerk continued:

> A possible solution may be to insist that the Department of the Interior appoint representatives at each of the principal ports. This department's function could then be confined to stopping every consignment of books, periodicals, etc marking the relative Landing and Delivery Orders "Detain pending release by Censorship. Customs requirements have been complied with." All the detail of examination and subsequent action could then be left to the representatives of Interior (in much the same way as detentions for Plant Inspector, Veterinarian, Health Officers, etc.).[44]

The last sentence is telling in terms of the logics by which Customs construed the task of reading. The content of publications is understood as a troublesome substance rather like a microbial disease that might lurk in plants, animals, or humans. Words constitute a type of viral thread that requires the expert eye and handling of a textual inspector (or indeed a literary examining officer like Hammett).

Through this epidemiological hermeneutic, seditious or obscene goods exuded microbial menace. Banned films were described as unfit for human consumption, objectionable condoms were deemed "harmful to health," indecent items were considered injurious to the public well-being, and undesirable publications apprehended in the post were likened to foreign bodies.[45] A logic of contamination and infection prevailed. In instances where one pirated piece of music or book was detected, the whole consignment came under suspicion and was generally detained.[46] These arguments could at times be turned against Customs: an importer whose periodicals had been detained argued that these publications were "perishables" and further detention would impair their freshness.[47]

THE GROWING ANTICOMMUNISM from the 1920s onward gave Customs further occasion to extend its scope. However, as the Cold War started to gain ground and as more films started to circulate (something for which Customs lacked viewing facilities), censorship was taken over by the Department of the Interior (with its specially built "censorship theatre") and then by an elaborate censorship apparatus set up in the early 1960s by the apartheid regime.[48] While there is a substantial body of scholarship on these censorship mechanisms, this scholarship, written during the apartheid era itself, has produced a somewhat monolithic grasp of the institution. More recently there have been attempts to disaggregate this view. Peter McDonald has traced the surprising sophistication of the early judgments of the apartheid censorship board in the early 1960s.[49] As he argues, this new censorship regime modeled itself in opposition to the crude methods of Customs, promising a more professional class of reader who had been recruited from the ranks of Afrikaner literary professors, some of them with newly minted doctorates in formalism from the Netherlands. These scholars had initially opposed the system but, when it became inevitable, had volunteered their services to try to save serious Afrikaans literature from the worst excesses of censorship. This idea of specialized and professional readers had in fact been used by the apartheid state to justify the introduction of its censorship board. The figure of the ham-handed Customs officer was invoked as the problem that had to be solved. Instead of these amateur readers, professionals would now be in charge of censorship.[50] Given the caliber of some of the literary scholars on the literature committee, some reports, especially in the early years, were remarkably sophisticated, as McDonald shows. One report on Gordimer's *The Late Bourgeois World* explored whether the novel's past tense narration made it more or less subversive.[51]

Yet, despite this new-look censorship, older Customs methods persisted. The first sign of this influence is in the preprinted forms used by the apartheid censors on the literary committee.[52] These were structured into four sections: (a) synopsis of publication dealt with; (b) references to pages on which appear passages considered to be indecent, obscene, or objectionable; (c) cover; and (d) general remarks and opinion. Section (b) in turn comprised a list of subcategories:

Crime
Violence
Description of murder
Sadism
Ill-treatment to women
Intimacies of women's bodies
Passionate love-making
Sexual relations
Loose morals
Traffic in drugs
White slave trade
The drug habit

Other vices
Offensive intermingling of European and Non-European
Other objectionable features (specify)
Subversive propaganda

While section (a) of the form encouraged censors to read and comment on the whole book, section (b) compelled them to read like Customs officers, sampling the text for objectionable portions. In addition, the inclusion of a comment on the cover of the book under section (c) echoes Customs methods of object-oriented reading (although most apartheid censors appear to have seldom taken up this option).

The censors' reports on J. M. Coetzee's *Waiting for the Barbarians* neatly capture the different reading strategies required by sections (a) and (b). Section (a) of the report by R. E. Lighton, a professor of English, provides a sophisticated discussion, highlighting the text's irony and Kafkaesque qualities while noting its complex exploration of themes of complicity. Section (b) comprises a list of page numbers as well as a swear-word count, with Lighton noting that the *f*-word is used eight times and that *shit* appears six times. Published by the London-based Secker and Warburg in 1980, *Waiting for the Barbarians* had in fact been referred to the Publication Control Board by Customs and Excise, another reminder of their lingering influence.[53]

One of the earliest objectives of this apartheid censorship machinery was to deal with seditious and obscene material produced inside South Africa, something that Customs censorship could not do, being focused solely on material coming from outside the country. As a system, apartheid itself aimed to locate, isolate, and, in some cases, exterminate internal dissidents. Edicts of banning played their part in this process, not only curtailing the circulation of ideas but also providing evidence by means of which writers could, in some instances, be prosecuted and imprisoned or driven into exile. Apartheid censorship placed the dissident author in its crosshairs, while drawing on a Customs-style hermeneutic of the book as an object of contamination.

Aiding these objectives was a powerful security and military apparatus that imprinted itself on censorship structures and protocols. It routinely referred books to the Publication Control Board, while its personnel peopled the censorship committees that dealt with security matters (the literature committee was a separate body). As McDonald has indicated, the literature committee maintained relatively sophisticated forms of reading, as opposed to the security committees, whose methods were more epidemiological, with one smidgeon of subversion enough to condemn a volume.⁵⁴ This military involvement in censorship had a long-standing history, stretching back to the opportunities that the Anglo-Boer War created for Customs to extend its reach. While scholars have examined aspects of military censorship during this war, its links to Customs and thence to the longer trajectories of censorship in South Africa have seldom been broached.

While the role of Customs has been noted in passing in histories of censorship in South Africa, this chapter has explored the insights that are generated if we insert Customs more prominently into these debates through tracing the genealogies of its methods of reading as these persisted across subsequent censorship regimes. Military styles of censorship, logistic reading, and an epidemiological orientation carried over into aspects of apartheid modes of censorship. These hermeneutical methods had emerged initially from the exigencies of the hydrocolonial frontier. Dockside reading had longer lives than one might initially anticipate.

Conclusion

Dockside Genres and Postcolonial Literature

In a recent collection entitled *Book Parts*, the editors observe that the book is "an alignment of separate component pieces, each possessed of particular conventions and histories."[1] This formulation presents the book as something of a cubist arrangement with parts angled in different directions. This image is a useful way to think about dockside reading. As books were transported by ship and moved through the colonial Custom House, they were disaggregated into their component parts: title, publisher, copyright inscription, cover, illustrations, language, script, contents. These parts were angled, or reangled in new directions, and in some cases, as with the markings on cargo, new sections were temporarily added.

Customs officials conferred new meanings on these component parts, orienting them in new directions. What were the longer-term implications of such reorientations? How did (or didn't) the protocols of the dockside carry over into literary practice beyond the port? This conclusion explores these themes in two steps: books and authorship and then genres of landing. The first examines how the various definitions of the book emerging from dockside reading shaped notions of authorship, while the second explores the trajectories of shipwreck narratives, port-city genres, and the farm novel.

Books and Authorship

Dockside reading produced several models of the book: as a charismatic object, as a species of stationery, as an epidemiological threat, and as a component of port infrastructure. The first arose out of dockside interpretations of copyright, the second out of Customs censorship, the third from the tariff, and the fourth from the daily use of Customs handbooks and manuals. All four models focused attention on the book rather than the author, who, in the first two instances, was so far away as to seem unreal. In the remaining cases, publications were generally authorless.

These models of intellectual production are manifest in different strands of southern African (and other postcolonial) literatures. In the case of the charismatic book, authorship was something that happened far away, generally in the metropolis, causing a relay of largely "white" writers to relocate to the imperial center as a precondition for a serious writing career. Much local writing, by contrast, remained a matter of filling out templates from elsewhere. The surviving copyright records from the Cape Colony bear out this profile: apart from serial publications and textbooks, the bulk of copyrighted material comprised handbooks, manuals, and form-like publications: Christmas annuals, letter-writing guides, cookbooks, seed catalogs, horse-training manuals, fruit growers' guides, farmers' yearbooks, ostrich feather–ready reckoners, handbooks for mounted infantry, bankers' and insurance agents' diaries, freemasons' directories, timetables, and tide tables.[2]

This use of boilerplating made sense in a context where books were rare and writing was shaped by the cut-and-paste methods of newspapers and periodicals.[3] As Stephanie Newell and Karin Barber have illustrated, the colonial newspaper provided an environment for experimenting with an imaginative range of writing and authorship positions that mobilized both print and oral genres (as the discussion of W. B. Rubusana has also indicated).[4] As Newell demonstrates, the British West African press was dominated by anonymous or pseudonymous forms of writing that allowed writers to evade, play with, and thwart the state's desire to classify and name its subjects, to make them legible and hence governable. Anonymity or pseudonymity offered a form of address that foregrounded the message, not the messenger, that severed text from body and hence offered an opportunity to speak as an abstract, disembodied subject. Oral forms and genres were enlisted in these experiments, with "folktales" appearing under cryptic or initialized attributions, the writer experimenting with the possibilities of yoking together a traditional form and "an author." As Barber demonstrates, oral forms and the genre of the periodical also discovered each other. The use of naming as an elaborated site of meaning and verbal creativity, a seminal component of oral poetry, expressed itself in the experiments with authorship in the press. The use of quotation or "quotedness," central to Yoruba praise poetry, likewise found an equivalent in the form of the periodical.

Epidemiological models of the book provided one indirect model for anticolonial and antiapartheid writers, who deployed books and pamphlets to confront authoritarian systems head-on. Given that such publications were often anonymous, this form of intellectual production focused attention on the text rather than the author. As an instrument of resistance, the book embodied notions of both charismatic power and epidemiological threat, in this instance not to its readers but to the state that sought to suppress it.

A further model of authorship, anti-imperial in orientation, took shape around port logistics and infrastructure and the larger systems of which they formed a part. For the Custom House, books were troublesome not only because they potentially contained objectionable content but also because they interrupted the logistic flow of goods through the port. Unsurprisingly, much anticolonial writing shaped itself around ideas of interruption (or counterlogistics, as the growing scholarship on logistics and containerization frames the issue today).[5] To take one famous example, Mohandas Gandhi's South African newspaper *Indian Opinion* fashioned itself as an instrument to slow down the industrial speed of empire and its logistics. As I have argued elsewhere, the methods of slow reading that Gandhi advocated became "one way of pausing industrial speed and in so doing, created small moments of intellectual independence. . . . This focus on bodily rhythm as a way of interrupting industrial tempos became central to his larger and world-famous critiques of modernity that questioned the equation of speed with efficiency and technology with progress."[6] In framing intellectual production in this way, Gandhi recognizes that to be in empire is to be bound to its systems of circulation and communication. Rather than positing a mode of opposition that could supposedly upend the system from outside, Gandhi took a more oblique approach, fostering practices of syncopated reading that could slow down the machine-driven rhythms of an industrial information order.

A final model is one that we might call authorship as landing, where writing functions to assist settler immigration but more specifically operates as an adjunct to port infrastructure to ensure a safe and dry landing for passengers of the right class and race. Most apparent in the settler handbook, this genre provided information on how to reach a particular colony, what to expect on arrival (often with the necessary forms included as appendices), and how to gain access to land or, as an Australian settler manual indicated, how to bring new arrivals "into touch with lands available for settlement."[7] Such handbooks played a prefatory part in the process of landing passengers. It can hence be considered a dockside genre, joining other texts like Customs manuals seeking to ensure the safe arrival of settlers (as well as their luggage), while acting in concert with submarine structures and wharfage mounted on reclaimed land. As an obviously hydrocolonial form of authorship, this genre is worth discussing in more detail.

Genres of Landing

Let us begin with a settler handbook by J. Forsyth Ingram, *The Story of an African Seaport: Being the History of the Port and Borough of Durban, the Seaport of Natal*. Published in 1899, the volume is aimed at merchants, businesspeople, and would-be settlers and describes "the commercial and maritime advantages that the Port possesses as an entrepot to the vast trade resources of the sub-Continent of Africa."[8] *The Story of an African Seaport* is one of several volumes by Ingram, all travel guides and handbooks, "which will be of practical utility alike to the settler and the traveller."[9] The book comprises three parts: the first sets out the history of the colony, the second focuses on the harbor (including a section on Customs and port regulations), and the third enumerates the amenities of the city itself while pointing to the various trajectories that settlers (all implicitly white and male) might follow in the colony.

Like many colonial accounts of the southeastern African seaboard, *The Story of an African Seaport* opens with tales of shipwreck, in this case three seventeenth-century disasters, the survivors of which furnished the first written accounts of the region. Especially in the prelongitude era, the southeastern littoral with its rough seas had long been notorious for shipwrecks, which have provided an enduring template in southern African literatures.[10] Colonial adventure novels often commence with a shipwreck, while castaway and captivity narratives continue to populate texts into the twenty-first century. These tropes initially attempt to overcome the anxiety that shipwreck presents to the imperial project while using the figure of white women castaways incorporated into African societies as a boundary marker of white male power.[11] More recently, writers have revisited these narrative forms in a postcolonial and post-apartheid mode, exploring shipwreck, captivity narrative, and whiteness as a pathological formation.[12]

Until recently, shipwreck writing did not register strongly in southern African literary histories, which understandably focused on land-based, national themes.[13] The oceanic turn has begun to change this situation, with coastal themes moving to the fore, suggesting ways of calibrating genres across land and sea.[14] Ingram's volume, and the settler handbook more generally, which straddle land and sea, are worth locating in these new littoral approaches.

The tripartite organization of Ingram's text moves from shipwreck, to port, to landed occupations. Brought into being by shipwreck but also overcoming and erasing it, the port plays a pivotal role, extending its infrastructure and artificial land into the ocean to enable a secure and dry landing for passengers and goods. Ingram's texts play a part in this process, extending a platform of advice and preparation to would-be settlers, inventing land for them before they arrive. Unsurprisingly, the infrastructure of the port features heavily with sections like "The Bluff and Signal Stations," "Dredging," and "Wharves and Wharf Extension."[15] In a companion volume, *The Colony of Natal* (1895), our attention is directed to "two celebrated piers or breakwaters." Ingram continues, "Probably no one who had enough interest in South Africa to read its history or its journals can be ignorant of the importance attached by the Colony and the shipping world to these two structures."[16] These two stalwart installations (along with dredging) had helped reduce the level of the sandbar and the shipwrecks that it occasioned. Ever-larger vessels were now able to enter the harbor, a scene almost obsessively represented in photographs, paintings, postcards, and periodicals.[17] Ingram adds his own version to this repertoire: "The day upon which these lines were penned saw a vessel of 3,000 tons come into the harbour and moor alongside the wharf without the slightest difficulty."[18]

In literary terms, we might say that Ingram sets up a relay among the story of the shipwreck, the port city, and the farm novel (one imagined end point of the settler's trajectory); the latter is inscribed in the title itself, which invokes Olive Schreiner's *The Story of an African Farm* (1883), the first South African novel to attract international attention (of which more later). In Ingram's railway/travel guides, the journey begins in the port city, and the reader/tourist is whisked inland by train, gliding by picturesque farmsteads that he (the implied reader is always male) may at some point occupy. The amenities of the port and the modern conveniences of the train system mean that the reader/tourist can experience the colonial adventure of arriving on the coast and moving into the interior without getting wet. The initial stages of the journey are marked episodically by features of harbor developments: "Lighthouse and Signal Station," "Breakwater and Bar," "The Wharves and Landing Facilities."[19] The process of creating artificial land, begun in the port, continues on the inland journey as Ingram invents landscapes and panoramas of settler habitation. We pass tea and sugar plantations, farmsteads, and mission stations; we hear about sheep and livestock, postal services, the water supply, and coal mines. Indigenous communities have all but disappeared: massacred, removed, or turned into ethnographic subjects who, like stoic statues, dot the narrative and its illustrations. Each node in the story, whether the plantation, farmstead, or mission station, provides a potential point of imaginative identification. The reader is hence offered a portfolio of narrative trajectories: the colonial adventure, the farm novel, the travelogue, the heroic mission story—all made possible by the port and the dry landing that its infrastructure enables. As Ben Mendelsohn remarks in another context, "Literature and land making are collaborative forces."[20]

The farm in Ingram's text is portrayed in terms of cost, climate, and crops and so may seem rather different from the farm novel with its concerns of romance and inheritance. Nonetheless, like the farm novel, Ingram's depictions operate as a potent narrative instrument of imaginative land possession (and dispossession), sharing some of the features of the genre outlined by J. M. Coetzee in his famed essay "Farm Novel and *Plaasroman*." Analyzing a range of examples (including Schreiner's novel), Coetzee demonstrates how the farm itself functions as a type of protagonist, with questions of who will marry whom and who will inherit subordinated to its larger design. The agent of the farm is its invariably male owner, who must act as a wise steward, an orientation that consecrates his possession of the land while erasing the dispossession on which it is premised.

Schreiner's text, by contrast, takes a different perspective, offering us an instance of the antifarm novel. The farm, set in the dry interior of the Cape Colony, is dominated by Tant' Sannie, a Boer matriarch, and Bonaparte Blenkins, an English itinerant schoolmaster, the one drawing on traditions of bonded labor, the other on traditions of imperial bullying. The craven nature of the pair is apparent from how they treat books, objects that excite deep suspicion. One day, Waldo, one of the three young protagonists, is discovered reading John Stuart Mill's *Principles of Political Economy*. Blenkins inspects the volume warily and

> soon came to a conclusion as to the nature of the book and its contents, by the application of a simple rule now largely acted upon, but which, becoming universal, would save much thought and valuable time. . . . Whenever you come into contact with any book, person, or opinion of which you absolutely comprehend nothing, declare that book, person or opinion to be immoral. Bespatter it, vituperate against it, strongly insist that any man or woman harbouring it is a fool or a knave, or both. Carefully abstain from studying it. Do all that in you lies to annihilate that book, person, or opinion.[21]

On hearing the title of the book, Tant' Sannie exclaims, "Dear Lord? Cannot one hear from the very sound what an ungodly book it is! One can hardly say the name. Haven't we got curses enough on this farm? . . . My best imported Merino ram dying of nobody knows what, and the short-horn cow casting her two calves, and the sheep eaten up with the scab and the drought?"[22]

Both behave rather like Customs examiners: Blenkins is determined to deal with the book without reading it, while Tant' Sannie regards the volume as an infectious substance that may bring further harm to the livestock. There is of course no suggestion of any direct link between Customs and these two reluctant readers, but their behavior offers a case of the epidemiological and authoritarian nature of port-city rule extending inland, strengthening the hands of bullies and tyrants. One is reminded of Keith Breckenridge's observation on the colonial state, which "began at the harbour, expanded to form the colonial city [and] followed the line of rail."[23] Ingram's texts reenact this trajectory, presenting this movement to the interior as the forward march of progress and white supremacy. The port city remains a key node in his narratives, trumping shipwreck and enabling settlers to become fully landed in all senses of the word. However, as colonial settler nationalism landed itself more thoroughly, these coastal trajectories were progressively erased. The farm novel has long been imagined as a dry form, far removed from the ocean. A view from the dockside helps us to recover some of its lost trajectories.

MUCH OF THIS BOOK was revised in Johannesburg during the COVID-19 lockdown, but as I was completing the manuscript in October 2020, things started to edge into some sort of normality. The university library cautiously reopened and listed as one of its health and safety provisions that returned books would be quarantined for seventy-two hours before being placed back on the shelves, a protocol recommended by several library associations.[24] The pandemic warped time and space, and the library's quarantine requirement momentarily seemed as if it might have come from the colonial Custom House itself. The book was once again an epidemiological object.

By October 2020, six months into the pandemic, paper as a site of infection had slipped fairly far down the list of possible danger zones. Nonetheless, one's early experience of the pandemic left a graphic sense of how alarming and alive a book might feel had it been exposed to the virus. Customs officials might have reacted in much the same way as consignments of publications were winched off infected ships. Yet, while this apprehension could be shared across time and space, one perception was peculiar to these examiners, namely, the idea that the words themselves were infected. At least one Australian official, as we have already noted, considered that the text itself was so contaminated that it could affect the pages on which it appeared, making censorship an act of solidarity with the paper itself.

With their ontological confusion, these adjudications produce an air of low comedy, rather like eating with a shoe or drinking from a sieve. Yet, rather than laugh at these officials, this book has taken that confusion as an analytic opportunity. As books crossed a hydrocolonial frontier, Customs examiners momentarily had to become book historians, pondering how to configure the inside and the outside of the book. Their default position was to trust the outside while downplaying the textual interior or treating it as infected. However, as a key substance of the book, the printed words insisted on being assayed in some way. Inspectors had to reach some accommodation with the inside of the book, which they did through their dockside hermeneutics. These were shaped hydrocolonially, by the elemental politics of the port, by the epidemiological and ideological prerogatives of the colonial maritime frontier, and by the books themselves. The definitions of bookhood that resulted were startlingly unusual—hopefully unusual enough to persuade other literary scholars to venture down to the dockside.

Notes

	ABBREVIATIONS
AG	Attorney-General
AGO	Attorney-General's Office
CKN	Collector of Customs, Knysna
CSO	Colonial Secretary's Office
DCU	Director of Customs
DEA	Customs and Excise
IDP	Interior Directorate of Publications
KAB	Cape Archives Depot/Kaapse Argiefbewaarplek
LD	Secretary to the Law Department
NAB	Natal Archives Depot/Natalse Argiefbewaarplek
NASA	National Archives of South Africa
SAB	Central Archives Depot/Sentrale Argiefbewaarplek
T	Treasury Department
TAB	Transvaal Archives Depot/Transvaalse Argiefbewaarplek
TES	Secretary of the Treasury

INTRODUCTION: HYDROCOLONIALISM

1. "Consolidated List of Prohibited and Restricted Imports and Exports Issued by Customs Departments," Trade Board, Cologne (HKE), II, T5/7, 1952–58, Central Archives Depot/Sentrale Argiefbewaarplek (SAB), National Archives of South Africa (NASA), Pretoria.
2. Oram, *Cargo Handling*, 12.
3. Conrad, *Mirror of the Sea*, 220, 195, 196, 21.
4. Terms from Gregory, *Tariffs*, 391, 394, 429.
5. Relevant here would be Margaret Smith's suggestion that the title page itself can be seen as emerging out of the logistics of transport, initially being a blank leaf used to

protect unbound quires during handling that then acquired a short "label-title" to identify the material. Smith, *Title-Page*, 47–58.

6   Details from "Contravention Customs Union Regulations. JE Bigwood—Standerton. 2 Cases Margarine . . . ," Director of Customs (DCU) 76, 670/06, 1906, Transvaal Archives Depot/Transvaalse Argiefbewaarplek (TAB), NASA, Pretoria; "Underentries of Duty: Foo Lee and Company. Tea Described as Herbs," DCU 85, 1416/06, 1906; and "H. Moschke, Pietersburg, Soup Squares, re Classification of," DCU 82, 1091/06, 1906.

7   "Importation of Poppy Seed," DCU 74, 574/06, 1906; and "'Gingham' (Flanelette) Tariff Item 175. Imported by Mosenthal Brothers, Limited," DCU 81, 1032/06, 1906.

8   Richard Wheatley, "The New York Custom-House," *Harper's New Monthly Magazine*, June 1884, 38–61.

9   "Merchandise Marks, Somaliland 1934," Colonial Office (CO) 535/101/10, National Archives, London. Thanks to Johan Mathew for this reference.

10 Oram, *Cargo Handling*, 12.

11 *General Instructions for the Landing-Waiters*.

12 For examples, see John McVey, "Cotton Codes," John McVey's website, accessed October 20, 2020, https://www.jmcvey.net/cable/cotton/index.htm.

13 Foucault, *Order of Things*, xvi. See also Duszat, "Foucault's Laughter."

14 Union of South Africa, *Customs Tariff* (1932), 130.

15 Bogost, *Alien Phenomenology*, 40–41.

16 Harman, *Tool-Being*, 247, 259.

17 Shaviro, *Universe of Things*, 32.

18 Jane Bennett, "Systems and Things," 227; see also Jane Bennett, *Vibrant Matter*.

19 Harman, *Tool-Being*, 295.

20 Behar, "Introduction to OOF." See also Tompkins, "On the Limits."

21 On the colonial state, see Breckenridge, *Biometric State*; and Cooper, *Africa since 1940*, 156–90. On South African immigration restrictions, see Dhupelia-Mesthrie, "False Fathers and False Sons"; Hyslop, "'Undesirable Inhabitants'"; MacDonald, "Strangers in a Strange Land"; and MacDonald, "Identity Thieves." On Australian immigration restrictions, see Martens, "Pioneering the Dictation Test?"; and Heath, *Purifying Empire*. On immigration restrictions internationally, see Lake and Reynolds, *Drawing the Global Colour Line*.

22 Barnes, "Cargo, 'Infection'"; Bashford, "Maritime Quarantine," 10; and L. Engelmann and Lynteris, *Sulphuric Utopias*. Thanks to Charne Lavery and Nolwazi Mkhwanazi for the last reference. See also Mawani, *Across Oceans of Law*, 120, which discusses how the manifest, a document pertaining to cargo, extended to control passengers and crew.

23 Orenstein, "Warehouses on Wheels," 653; Dalbello, "Reading Immigrants," 179–90; and Ellis Island Immigration Museum, "The Inspection Process," accessed December 3, 2019, http://www.bringinghistoryhome.org/assets/bringinghistoryhome/2nd-grade/unit-2/EllisIsland_14.htm. My thanks to Marija Dalbello for drawing her work to my attention.

24 "Merchandise Marks Law," Collector of Customs, Knysna (CKN) 3/9, 128/6/4, 1910–36, Cape Archives Depot/Kaapse Argiefbewaarplek (KAB), NASA, Cape Town; and "Prohibited and Restricted Imports. Indecent and Objectionable Articles," Customs and Excise (DEA) 199, A10/5X, 1958, SAB, NASA, Pretoria.
25 Harney and Moten, *Undercommons*.
26 South African Railways and Harbours, *Official Railway Tariff Handbook*; Union of South Africa, *Customs Tariff* (1932); and Union of South Africa, *Customs Tariff* (1936).
27 Department of Commercial Intelligence and Statistics, India, *Indian Customs Tariff*, table of contents.
28 Gitelman, *Paper Knowledge*, 52.
29 I am indebted to Geeta Patel for this point about assaying.
30 Coghlan, *Customs Manual*.
31 Duncan, "Indexes."
32 For an example with a waterproof cover, see *Instructions to Preventive Men* in the British Library; for extra pages, see Lewis, *South African Customs Union Tariff*; and, for interleaving, see South African Railways and Harbours, *Official Railway Tariff Handbook*.
33 Clements, *Clements' Customs Pocket Manual*; *Tariff Dictionary*; and Bengal, Customs Department, *Calcutta Customs Calculation Manual*.
34 *Wine and Spirit Merchant's Assistant*; and Clements, *Customs Guide*.
35 Viswanathan, *Masks of Conquest*.
36 "City of Johannesburg. City Health Department. Disinfection of Library Books," Public Health Johannesburg/Staatsgesondheid Johannesburg (SGJ) 96, 4/25/3, 1915–43, SAB, NASA, Pretoria.
37 Hofmeyr, *Portable Bunyan*, 25–28.
38 *Tariff Dictionary*, 21; and "Prohibited and Restricted Imports. Objectionable Literature," DEA 200, A10/6X, 1950–52.
39 For Australian examples, see Adelaide Intelligence and Tourist Bureau, *South Australia*; and New South Wales, Intelligence Department, *New South Wales*. For a South African instance, see Ingram, *Story of an African Seaport*.
40 My thanks to Smaran Dayal and Claire Soh, who first pointed out the idea of thinking about literature as land reclamation.
41 Titlestad, *Shipwreck Narratives*.
42 Coetzee, "Farm Novel and *Plaasroman*."
43 My thanks to Trev Broughton and Sally Shuttleworth for these examples. Bell, *Villette*, 57.
44 Waugh, *Vile Bodies*, 22.
45 Hawthorne, *Scarlet Letter*, 39.
46 Crain, *Story of A*, 183–84.
47 McGill, *American Literature*, 218–69.
48 Nadine Gordimer, letter to the Secretary of the Interior, January 23, 1973, Nadine Gordimer Collection, A 3367, F 3, Censorship in South Africa, Historical Papers, University of the Witwatersrand, Johannesburg.

49 Graeber, *Utopia of Rules*, 26–29; Hull, *Government of Paper*; and Hoag and Hull, *Review of the Anthropological Literature*. Comments on the algorithm and bureaucrats are extrapolated from Dietrich, "Algorithm."
50 Price, *How to Do Things with Books*; Mukhopadhyay, "On Not Reading"; Hsiung, "Knowledge Made Cheap"; and Gitelman, "Not."
51 Stewart, *Bookwork*, 7.
52 For earlier discussions of the term, see Hofmeyr and Bystrom, "Oceanic Routes"; and Hofmeyr, "Provisional Notes on Hydrocolonialism." See also the special issue on hydrocriticism edited by Laura Winkiel: *English Language Notes* 57, no. 1 (2019).
53 I am grateful to Luck Makuyana for drawing the question of flooding as colonization to my attention.
54 Pritchard, "From Hydroimperialism to Hydrocapitalism," 591.
55 Mosse, *Rule of Water*; Fontein, "Power of Water"; McKittrick, "Making Rain, Making Maps"; Hughes, "Hydrology of Hope"; and Swyngedouw, *Liquid Power*.
56 Quotation from S. Engelmann, "Towards a Poetics of Air," 430.
57 Linton and Budds, "Hydrosocial Cycle."
58 Da Cunha, *Invention of Rivers*, blurb and p. x. See also da Cunha and Mathur, *Soak*.
59 There is extensive scholarship on this topic. A standard work is Pearson, *Indian Ocean*.
60 Ghosh, *In an Antique Land*; Gurnah, *By the Sea*; and Collen, *Mutiny*. See also Lavery, "Writing the Indian Ocean."
61 Issur, "Postcolonial Narratives." On floods, see Posmentier, *Cultivation and Catastrophe*, 132–57; and Jones, "'As If the Water.'"
62 "Insularity and Internationalism: An Interview with Kaiama L. Glover," The Public Archive: Black History in White Times, June 4, 2013, https://thepublicarchive.com/?p=3881. See also Deckard, "Political Ecology of Storms."
63 The classic study is Lan, *Guns and Rain*.
64 Nuttall, "Pluvial Time/Wet Form," 456.
65 Gillis, *Human Shore*.
66 Samuelson, "Coastal Form"; and Allen, Groom, and Smith, *Coastal Works*.
67 Samuelson, "Coastal Form," 17.
68 M. Cohen, "Chronotopes of the Sea," 649.
69 Ghosh, *Hungry Tide*; Okorafor, *Lagoon*; and Martel, *Life of Pi*.
70 Alaimo, "Violet-Black"; and Joshua Bennett, "Beyond the Vomiting Dark."
71 Walcott, "The Sea Is History," 364–7.
72 M. NourbeSe Philip, "Wor(l)ds Interrupted: The Unhistory of the Kari Basin," *Jacket2*, September 17, 2013, https://jacket2.org/article/worlds-interrupted, which mentions Césaire's use of volcanic images.
73 See Lavery's section "Deep Histories of the Indian Ocean" in Isabel Hofmeyr and Charne Lavery, "Exploring the Indian Ocean as a Rich Archive of History—above and below the Water Line," The Conversation, June 7, 2020, https://theconversation.com/exploring-the-indian-ocean-as-a-rich-archive-of-history-above-and-below-the-water-line-133817.

74 Pritchard, "From Hydroimperialism to Hydrocapitalism."
75 Swyngedouw, *Liquid Power*, 43.
76 Graber, "Flow Dynamics."
77 Dickens, *Great Expectations*; Serpell, *Old Drift*.
78 This is the research focus of Oceanic Humanities for the Global South, accessed October 20, 2020, http://www.oceanichumanities.com.
79 Blum, *View from the Mast-Head*; and M. Cohen, *Novel and the Sea*.
80 Killingray, "Introduction," 5.
81 Delmas, "From Travelling to History"; Hyslop, "Guns, Drugs and Revolutionary Propaganda"; Liebich, "Connected Readers"; and Maynard, "'In the Interests of our People.'" My thanks to Samia Khatun for the last reference.
82 Rudy, *Imagined Homelands*; and Shaikh, "*The Alfred* and *The Open Sea*."
83 Starosielski, "Elements of Media Studies"; and McCormack, *Atmospheric Things*, 4. For a postcolonial angle, see Allewaert, "Super Fly," which can be read as an elemental approach to the materiality of colonial documents.
84 Peters, *Marvelous Clouds*, 1, 14; see also J. Cohen and Duckert, *Elemental Ecocriticism*.
85 Jue, *Wild Blue Media*, 7.
86 Taylor, *Sky of Our Manufacture*, 7.
87 Carroll, *Empire of Air and Water*, 6. See also Hensley and Steer, "Ecological Formalism."
88 Pertinent here would be the Blue (or Salt) Water principle that was debated in the United Nations in the 1950s and 1960s. This motion argued that for any unit to be defined as a colony (and hence to be eligible for decolonization), it needed to be separated from its colonizing power by at least thirty miles of seawater. Initiated by the Organization of African Unity and supported by the United States, the motion sought to counter attempts by Belgium, in the process of resentfully relinquishing the Congo, to extend definitions of decolonization to ethnic, indigenous, and "tribal" groups who could claim internal and land-based forms of colonization, whether by the Belgians or the new postcolonial regime. The principle enabled a narrow definition of colonization that shored up the authority of the nation-state. My thanks to Bruce Robbins for bringing this point to my attention. Robbins, "Blue Water: A Thesis," 2015, Bruce Robbins's website, http://blogs.cuit.columbia.edu/bwr2001/files/2016/02/Robbins.Blue-Water.pdf. There have been attempts to use the sea or, in this case, the seabed for anti-imperial purposes. As Anna Zalik's work on the International Seabed Authority demonstrates, this body has attempted to reanimate a "Bandung era discourse that frames the deep sea as the 'common heritage of humankind.'" Zalik, "Deep Seabed and Colonial Redress," quote from abstract. Also relevant is DeLoughrey, "Toward a Critical Ocean Studies."
89 DeLoughrey, "Toward a Critical Ocean Studies," 22, 27.
90 DeLoughrey, "Toward a Critical Ocean Studies," 26.
91 Colony of Natal, Natal Harbour Department, *Regulations of the Port*.
92 Mendelsohn, "Making the Urban Coast," 457.

93 Jue, "Submerging Kittler."

94 On diving, see Jue, "Wild Blue Media," 1–12. Stacy Alaimo's page on Academia.edu features a picture of her snorkeling; accessed December 2, 2019, https://uta.academia.edu/StacyAlaimo. On "thinking with," see Hayward, "More Lessons from a Starfish"; see "coral imaginaries" from Khal Torabully, discussed in Ette, "Khal Torabully." On submarine aesthetics, see DeLoughrey, "Submarine Futures of the Anthropocene." For a range of underwater artists, dancers, and sculptors, see "Art beneath the Waves," *Pursuit of Beauty*, BBC Radio 4, last aired April 6, 2019, https://www.bbc.co.uk/programmes/m00013nr. See also M. Cohen, "Seeing through Water."

95 On speculative fictions, see Chan, "'Alive . . . Again'"; on underwater photography, see M. Cohen, "Underwater Imagination"; on aquariums and coral reefs, see Elias, *Coral Empire*, 125–26; on rococo decoration, see Quigley, "Porcellaneous Ocean"; on shipwrecks, see M. Cohen, "Shipwreck as Undersea Gothic"; two examples of oceanically linked conceptual poetry include M. NourbeSe Philip's *Zong!* and Caroline Bergvall's *Drift*; on harbor engineering, see Hofmeyr, "Imperialism."

96 Hofmeyr, "Imperialism." On the harbor floor method, see "The Floor of Sydney Harbour," Sydney Environment Institute, University of Sydney, January 24, 2018, https://sei.sydney.edu.au/research/oceans/floor-sydney-harbour/; and Dredge Research Collective, "Mapping New York Harbor," September 2012, https://dredgeresearchcollaborative.org/works/mapping-new-york-harbor/.

97 Vahed, "Mosques, Mawlanas and Muharram"; and Vahed, "Constructions of Community and Identity."

98 Bernard, "Messages from the Deep." On Khoisan beliefs, see de Prada-Samper, "'Partial Clue'" (my thanks to John Parkington for this reference). On Muslim water jinn, see "Djin-Vrou" (my thanks to Saarah Jappie for this reference); and on "watermeisie" (water girl/spirit), see Mohulatsi, "Black Aesthetics."

99 On aquafuturism, see Chan, "'Alive . . . Again.'"

100 "Ellen Gallagher," Hauser and Wirth, accessed December 5, 2019, https://www.hauserwirth.com/artists/2783-ellen-gallagher; Sharpe, *In the Wake*; and Wikipedia, s.v. "Drexciya," accessed December 9, 2020, https://en.wikipedia.org/wiki/Drexciya. See also Philip, *Zong!*; Finney, "Undersea World of Jacques Cousteau"; Finney, "Shark Bite" (my thanks to Evie Shockley for making me aware of Finney's poems); and Nia Love, "g1(host): lostatsea," Gibney Company Community Center, November 7, 2019, https://gibneydance.org/event/nia-love-g1host-lostatsea/2019-11-07/ (my thanks to Greg Vargo for the last reference).

101 Oupa Sibeko's "Bottled Seawater: A Sea Inland" explores intersections between African ancestral beliefs and Atlantic slavery, a theme also touched on in Koleka Putuma's "Water" in *Collective Amnesia*. For performances of "Water," see "Koleka Putuma—Water," October 2015, YouTube video, 6:48, https://www.youtube.com/watch?v=UGdqcEKlGhw; and "Koleka Putuma—Water (Official Video)," June 27, 2016, YouTube video, 7:09, https://www.youtube.com/watch?v=8dfq3C8GNrE. See also Baderoon, "African Oceans."

102 Bergemann, "Council of (In)Justice," appendix, "1730s Criminal Database," case of Rijkaert Jacobsz and Claas Bank.
103 Schmidt, *Death Flight*; and Guzmán, *Pearl Button*.
104 Sato, "'Operation Legacy'"; and Wikipedia, s.v. "Operation Legacy," accessed December 5, 2020, https://en.wikipedia.org/wiki/Operation_Legacy.
105 "Collector of Customs Wharf Accommodation at the Port," Colonial Secretary's Office (CSO) 595, 1877/1971, 1877, Natal Archives Depot/Natalse Argiefbewaarplek (NAB) NASA, Pietermaritzburg; "Collector of Customs Department. Messrs Harlem, Hooper and Mahoney Forward a Memorial on the Subject of Their Salaries," CSO 676, 1878/1394, 1878; and "Collector of Customs Says a Minute Paper from Colonial Office, in Reference to Custom House Premises Has Been Lost . . . ," CSO 676, 1878/1121, 1878.

1: THE CUSTOM HOUSE AND HYDROCOLONIAL GOVERNANCE

1 For a detective novel, see Seymour, *Untouchable*.
2 On England, see Ashworth, *Customs and Excise*; on the United States, see Rao, *National Duties*; see also the "biography" of the Custom House: Rideout, *Custom House*; and, on the Dublin Custom House, Robins, *Custom House People*. There is a small South African scholarship on the Customs Union and from economic historians working on taxation. Van der Poel, *Railway and Customs Policies*; Bruwer, *Protection in South Africa*; De Kock, *Selected Subjects*; Basson, "Regte op invoere"; and Colesky, "Comparative Study."
3 Ashworth, *Customs and Excise*.
4 Ashworth, *Customs and Excise*, 147.
5 "George Rutherford Esquire, Collector of Customs Applies for Permission to Retire from the Service in August Next," CSO 1212, 1888/C24, 1888; "Colonial Secretary re Pension to G Rutherford Esquire, Charles, Michael and George, on His Retirement from the Post of Collector of Customs," CSO 1211, 1889/862, 1889; and "George Rutherford Encloses a Letter Addressed to the Crown Agents on the Subject of His Pension, Which He Requests May Be Forwarded through This Office," CSO 1233, 1889/5266, 1889.
6 Da Silva et al., "Diaspora of Africans"; and Adderley, *"New Negroes from Africa,"* 42–43. On Cape Town, see McKenzie, "Daemon behind the Curtain"; and Shell, "Introduction."
7 Atton and Holland, *King's Customs*, 142, 153.
8 Carson, "Customs Plantation Records."
9 George Rutherford to G. Matthews, June 1, 1859, George Rutherford Collection, National Library of South Africa, Cape Town. Despite its rather grand-sounding title, this collection comprises only one letter.
10 Desai and Vahed, *Inside Indian Indenture*, 62.
11 Ellis, "Impact of White Settlers," 39.
12 Theal, *Records of the Cape Colony*, 27:226.

13   "Collector of Customs Asking That the Controller of Arms May Be Allowed to Use His Discretion with Regard to the Destruction of Certain Old Guns and Pistols in the Office of the Collector of Customs," CSO 944, 1884/188, 1884; "Rutherford, Custom House re Revolvers of Proudfoot," Attorney-General's Office (AGO) I/9/1, 18A/1863, 1863, NAB, NASA, Pietermaritzburg; "Collector of Customs Certain Firearms Not Realising the Reserve Amount of Duty Placed on Them Were Not Sold at the Sale . . . ," Natal Treasury 64, T908/1896, 1896, NAB, NASA, Pietermaritzburg; and "Rutherford, Custom House Declares Possession of Jewellry and Cigars Seized for Breach of Custom Ordinance," AGO I/9/4, 8A/1879, 1879.

14   Searchy, *Custom House Handbook*, 14–19, quotation from 14.

15   Wilson, *Flags at Sea*, 41, 9.

16   "Collector of Customs Says a Minute Paper from Colonial Office, in Reference to Custom House Premises Has Been Lost . . . ," CSO 676, 1878/1121, 1878.

17   Hein, "Port Cities," 813.

18   "Collector of Customs Wharf Accommodation at the Port," CSO 595, 1877/1971, 1877; "Collector of Customs Department. Messrs Harlem, Hooper and Mahoney Forward a Memorial on the Subject of Their Salaries," CSO 676, 1878/1394, 1878; and "Collector of Customs Says a Minute Paper from Colonial Office, in Reference to Custom House Premises Has Been Lost . . . ," CSO 676, 1878/1121, 1878.

19   "Collector of Customs Says a Minute Paper from Colonial Office, in Reference to Custom House Premises Has Been Lost . . . ," CSO 676, 1878/1121, 1878; see also "Collector of Customs Wharf Accommodation at the Port," CSO 595, 1877/1971, 1877.

20   "The Collector of Customs: Charles Spradbrow, Customs Watchman, Requests a Site May Be Granted Him on Which to Build a Cottage," CSO 601, 1877/2579, 1877; and Hawthorne, *Scarlet Letter*, 13.

21   On regiments, see "The Collector of Customs States That Mr Tyrrell, Member of the Durban Mounted Rifles, and a Clerk in His Department, Is Absent from His Post," CSO 674, 1878/4473, 1878; on sports teams, see photographs: "Cricket Team with Trophy—Department of Trade and Customs Staff," NAA: A3560, 1142, 3117648; and "Her Majesty's Customs Football Team," NAA: D5063, 737, 3401652, both in the National Archives of Australia, Canberra.

22   *Tide-Waiting, a Poem*.

23   "John Davies, Clerk of the Peace, Durban: Enclosing Deposition of the Collector of Customs in Which a Ship's Captain Did Not Find Him Sleeping Room below Deck as the Law Says He Must," AGO I/8/10, 334A/1868, 1868.

24   "Collector of Customs. Removal of 'Long Room' from Point to Durban," CSO 782, 1880/4791, 1880.

25   Fletcher, *London Custom House*, 8.

26   Ashworth, *Customs and Excise*, loc. 4692 of 6832.

27   "George Rutherford, CMG, Asks for a Sketch Plan of the Proposed Harbour Improvements," Minister of Justice and Public Works 87, LW 4702/1901, 1901, NAB, NASA, Pietermaritzburg.

28 Natal (Colony), Commission on the Port and Harbour of Natal, *Report and Second Interim Report*, 28.
29 Hofmeyr, *Gandhi's Printing Press*, 30.
30 Quoted in Natal Indian Congress Memorial to Secretary of State for the Colonies, March 15, 1897, in Gandhi, *Collected Works*, 2:36. Thanks to Goolam Vahed for this reference.
31 Bender, *Who Saved Natal?*; and Heydenrych, "Port Natal Harbour."
32 Bender, *Who Saved Natal?*, 73, 104, 91; Harry Escombe Papers, A 159.5, file 5, NAB, NASA, Pietermaritzburg; and Cathcart William Methven, *Sketches of Durban and Its Harbour*, 1891, Wikimedia Commons, accessed December 5, 2020, https://commons.wikimedia.org/wiki/Category:Sketches_of_Durban_and_its_Harbour_(1891)_by_C._W._METHUEN.
33 Bernard, "Messages from the Deep."
34 Agius, "Red Sea Folk Beliefs."

2: CUSTOMS AND OBJECTS ON A HYDROCOLONIAL FRONTIER

1 Gregory, *Tariffs*; Higginson, *Tariffs at Work*; McGuire, *British Tariff System*; and *Tariff Dictionary*.
2 "Customs and Excise. Inspection Report. Collector of Customs, Cape Town," Public Service Commission 25, 4/3/8, 1922–30, SAB, NASA, Pretoria; and McGuire, *British Tariff System*.
3 The taxonomies of tariff schedules varied by country and period. By the mid-nineteenth century, an alphabetical system had given way to an animal, vegetable, and mineral grid. Asakura, *World History*, 211–13.
4 South African Railways and Harbours, *Official Railway Tariff Handbook*.
5 Details from "Contravention Customs Union Regulations. JE Bigwood—Standerton. 2 Cases Margarine . . . ," DCU 76, 670/06, 1906; "Underentries of Duty: Foo Lee and Company. Tea Described as Herbs," DCU 85, 1416/06, 1906; "H. Moschke, Pietersburg, Soup Squares, re Classification of," DCU 82, 1091/06, 1906; "Re Duty Leviable on 'Gloy,'" DCU 71, 415/06, 1906; "Importation of Poppy Seed," DCU 74, 574/06, 1906; and "'Gingham' (Flanelette) Tariff Item 175. Imported by Mosenthal Brothers, Limited," DCU 81, 1032/06, 1906.
6 "Butter Paper—re Duty Leviable," DCU 97, 379/07, 1907; "Prohibited and Restricted Imports Trade and Merchandise Marks. Precedent," DEA 205, A10/18X, 1927–33; "Handmade Paper Entered as Printing Paper, Duty Free," DCU 72, 465/06, 1906; and "Classification of Labels for Sheep's Ear," DCU 67, 202/06, 1906.
7 Jane Bennett, *Vibrant Matter*, 94, quoting Charles Darwin.
8 "Control of Railway and Water Enquiry into Working of Water Police," Secretary of Justice (JUS) 891, 1/391/25, 1914–29, TAB, NASA, Pretoria; and "Regarding Enquiry into Working of the Water Police," South African Police (SAP) 7, CONF 6/115/13, 1912–13, SAB, NASA, Pretoria.
9 Examples from Stevens, *On the Stowage*, 86, 164, 120, 68, 70–71.

10 Callebert, "Livelihood Strategies," 168.
11 "Report and Manifest of the Cargo Laden aboard the Ship Chelsea," February 23, 1828, reproduced in Douglas L. Stein, "Manifest," in *American Maritime Documents, 1776–1860*, Mystic Seaport Museum, 1992, https://research.mysticseaport.org/item/loo6405/loo6405-c026/.
12 Vandenabeele, Bertels, and Wouters, "Baltic Shipping Marks." For an example of such a manual, see *The Timber Trades Journal List of Shipping Marks*.
13 See John McVey, "Cotton Codes," John McVey's website, accessed October 20, 2020, https://www.jmcvey.net/cable/cotton/index.htm.
14 Morshead, *Merchandise Marks Manual*, 35–36.
15 Thanks to Charne Lavery for this phrase.
16 Ernest E. Williams, "The Contentious Mark," *Saturday Review*, September 18, 1897, 313; and Minchinton, "E. E. Williams."
17 "Prohibited and Restricted Imported Trade and Merchandise Marks. Precedent. Customs and Excise," DEA 205, A10/18X, 1927–33.
18 Morshead, *Merchandise Marks Manual*; and Wakefield, *Foreign Marks*.
19 Wakefield, *Foreign Marks*, 22.
20 The verbs and adverbs are culled from a range of pages in Wakefield, *Foreign Marks*.
21 Kerly and Underday, *Law of Trade-Marks*, 826.
22 Wakefield, *Foreign Marks*, 83.
23 "Importation of Poppy Seed," DCU 74, 574/06, 1906.
24 On the lady's trimmed hat, see CKN 3/15, T 14, 1936–40. On the slippers, see "Customs Dues and Excise," CKN 3/1, 64, 1909–36.
25 "German Prints," DCU 82, 1072/06, 1906.
26 "Selampores," DCU 82, 1074/06, 1906.
27 "Selampores," DCU 82, 1074/06, 1906.
28 "Printed and Calicos," DCU 81, 1022/06, 1906.
29 "Interpretations of the Tariff," DCU 79, 987/07, 1907.

3: COPYRIGHT ON A HYDROCOLONIAL FRONTIER

1 Sayer, *Homeward-Bound Passenger's Companion*, 10.
2 My thanks to Meredith McGill for explaining the significance of this date.
3 Sayer, *Homeward-Bound Passenger's Companion*, 10–11, 36.
4 Bently, "'Extraordinary Multiplicity.'"
5 "Prohibited Imports. Copyright Works," DEA 202, A10/8X, 1915–61.
6 Seville, *Internationalisation of Copyright Law*; Bently, "Copyright, Translations"; Peukert, "Colonial Legacy"; and Rukavina, *Development of the International Book Trade*. Michael Birnhack's *Colonial Copyright*, unlike the preceding works, explores the social life of copyright law. For the South African history, see Dean, "Application of the Copyright Act."
7 To complicate matters further, the Customs Act of the same year outlawed the importation of any book printed without permission but specified that this con-

dition applied only to Britain, leaving out any mention of the dominions, an oversight only corrected in 1845. Ronan Deazley, "Commentary on *Foreign Reprints Act* 1847," Primary Sources on Copyright (1450–1900), ed. Lionel Bently and Martin Kretschmer, 2008, http://www.copyrighthistory.org/cam/tools/request/showRecord?id=commentary_uk_1847.

8. Seville, *Internationalisation of Copyright Law*, 86–90.
9. Evidence of Charles Trevelyan, in *Royal Commission on Copyright: Minutes of Evidence*, London (1878), available online: Primary Sources on Copyright (1450–1900), ed. Lionel Bently and Martin Kretschmer, 1. http://www.copyrighthistory.org/cam/tools/request/showRepresentation?id=representation_uk_1878a.
10. "British Copyright Works," DCU 67, 237/06, 1906–10.
11. "Duty on Copyright Works," CSO 1213, 1889/1320, 1889.
12. "Prohibited Imports. Copyright Works," DEA 202, A10/8X, 1915–61.
13. "Prohibited Imports. Copyright Works," DEA 202, A10/8X, 1915–61.
14. Kerly and Underday, *Law of Trade-Marks*, 823.
15. Payn, *Merchandise Marks Act*, 10, 11.
16. Morshead, *Merchandise Marks Manual*, 19.
17. Payn, *Merchandise Marks Act*, 11.
18. Payn, *Merchandise Marks Act*, 78. General order issued by the commissioners of customs for the carrying out of the Merchandise Marks Act of 1887.
19. "Prohibited Imports. Copyright Works," DEA 202, A10/8X, 1915–61.
20. "Seizure under the Copyright Protection and Books Registration Act of 1895 of Certain Books," Treasury Department (T) 972, 936, 1906, KAB, NASA, Cape Town.
21. "Customs—Detention of Certain Books by the Johannesburg Customs Authorities," Governor of the Transvaal Colony 974, GOV, PS 21/7/06, 1906, TAB, NASA, Pretoria.
22. "Prohibitions," CKN 3/8, 23/6/2, 1921.
23. "Re Importations of American Encyclopaedia Britannica—Stated to Be a Pirated Copy of the English One," DCU 115, 545, 1908.
24. "Prohibited Imports. Copyright Works," DEA 202, A10/8X, 1915–61.
25. "Prohibited Imports. Copyright Works," DEA 202, A10/8X, 1915–61.
26. Dean, "Application of the Copyright Act," 256–57.
27. "Copyright Bill," CSO 1457, 1084/1896, 1896.
28. "Prohibition Copyright Work," DEA 202, A10/8X, 1916.
29. "Annual Report 1926. The Registrar of Patents, Designs, Trade Marks and Copyright and of Companies," Secretary of Justice 417, 1/589/26, 1925–26.
30. "Prohibited and Restricted Imports. Trade and Merchandise Marks. Precedent," DEA 205, A10/8X, 1939–52.
31. "Prohibited Imports. Copyright Works," DEA 202, A10/8X, 1915–61.
32. Payn, *Merchandise Marks Act*, 22. For a comparative view on trademarks in India, see Rajagopal, "Early Publicity in India."
33. Wakefield, *Foreign Marks*, 85.
34. Wakefield, *Foreign Marks*, 67–68.

35 "Prohibitions," CKN 3/8, 23/6/2, 1910–36.
36 Saunders, "Copyright, Obscenity and Literary History."
37 Duguid, "Information in the Mark." Also relevant would be Harris, "Whiteness as Property"; and Vats and Keller, "Critical Race IP."
38 Peukert, "Colonial Legacy," 40.
39 "Copyright Act," Secretary of Native Affairs 1930, 202/278, 1932–37, SAB, NASA, Pretoria.
40 Relevant here is Stephen Best, who sees intellectual property law as arising from the ongoing "crisis involving the subjection of personhood to property." Best, *Fugitive's Properties*, loc. 262 of 5594. See also Harris, "Whiteness as Property."
41 McGill, "Copyright," 199.
42 Copyright's limited traction is apparent if one turns to Paul Saint-Amour, who has traced how modernist works register an awareness of their own status as intellectual property in their structure and architecture. Saint-Amour, *Copywrights*. This question has not been asked in relation to southern African literature (and indeed postcolonial literature more generally) but would be a productive route to follow. Given the modest reach of copyright, I am aware of only one South African novel that explicitly addresses this theme. Written by the leading legal academic on copyright in the country, Owen Dean's *The Summit Syndrome* is a murder mystery, hinging on the plagiarism of a law textbook.
43 Scardamaglia, "Colonial Trade Mark Regime," 278, 283.
44 "Patents, Designs, Trade Marks and Copyright," Department of Trade and Industry (HEN) 2334, 437/1/29, 1950–52, NASA, Pretoria.
45 This account is drawn from "Broadcasting: Honours: Salutes. Resolution Passed by the Transvaal Listener's Association Protesting against the Unauthorised and Unofficial Use of 'Die Stem' as the South African Nation Anthem . . . ," Governor-General 245, 3/5499, 1938, SAB, NASA, Pretoria; "Legislation: 'Stem van Suid-Africa' Copyright Act, 1959 . . . ," Governor-General 478, 7/6807, 1959; and "National Anthem of the Union of South Africa," Secretary for Foreign Affairs 55/44, 1933–42, and 55/44/1, 1943–53, SAB, NASA, Pretoria.
46 For Cape figures, see Deeds Registry Office, "Transcript of the Entries Registered in the Registry Book under Acts. No. 2 of 1873 and 4 of 1888 . . . Published in Terms of Section VI of the Last Mentioned Act," MSB729, 1894–1901, South African Library, Cape Town. For brief mention of Natal figures, see "Copyright in the Empire," Prime Minister (PM) 74, 1908/1026, 1908, NASA, Pietermaritzburg, which gives the number from 1897 to 1910 as 183 entries, on average 14 per annum. The Transvaal Colony's *Government Gazette* carries figures from 1910 to 1916, with an average of twenty-five entries per year. The archives of the Secretary to the Law Department (LD) carry some copyright registration records: see, for example, "Registration of Copyright—February 1905," LD 1032, 1108/05, 1905, TAB, NASA, Pretoria; "Registration of Copyright—June 1905," LD 1101, 2978/05, 1905; and "Registration of Copyright—May 1906," LD 253, 34/06, 1906.

47 Hofmeyr, *Gandhi's Printing Press*, 39; and Vail and White, *Power and the Praise Poem*, 3–39.
48 On this point, see Kraut, *Choreographing Copyright*. For a different perspective, on queer writers questioning the structures of intellectual property, see Irr, *Pink Pirates*. On the question of credentialing and imperial citizenship, see Banerjee, *Becoming Imperial Citizens*. See also Harris, "Whiteness as Property."
49 For questions of anticolonial authorship in British West Africa, see Newell, *Power to Name*. For a Nigerian perspective, see Barber, "Authorship, Copyright and Quotation."
50 Rubusana, *Zemk'inkomo magwalandini*. The translations are drawn from Opland, *Xhosa Poets and Poetry*, 64; *The Greater Dictionary of isiXhosa*; and "Dr. Walter Rubusana," South African History Online, produced February 17, 2011, last updated February 18, 2021, http://www.sahistory.org.za/people/dr-walter-benson-rubusana.
51 Peires, "Lovedale Press"; and White, "Lovedale Press."
52 Woodmansee, "Genius and the Copyright"; Jaszi, "Towards a Theory of Copyright"; Pettitt, *Patent Inventions*; and Rose, *Authors and Owners*. For a different perspective, see McGill, "Copyright and Intellectual Property"; and Bracha, "Ideology of Authorship Revisited." For an Australian perspective, see Scardamaglia, "Colonial Trade Mark Regime," 278, 283.
53 Johns, *Nature of the Book*, 213–65.

4: CENSORSHIP ON A HYDROCOLONIAL FRONTIER

1 Heath, *Purifying Empire*, 123.
2 Melville, *Moby Dick*, 2.
3 Quotations are from the section "The Censorship Office" in "Customs House," Immigration Museum, Museums Victoria, accessed December 5, 2019, https://museumsvictoria.com.au/longform/customs-house/.
4 Gordimer, letter to the Secretary of the Interior, January 23, 1973, Nadine Gordimer Collection, A 3367, F 3.
5 Gordimer, "Censorship and the Artist," 12.
6 These comments resonate with Sigmund Freud's description of the superego as a Customs inspector, policing what may pass across the border of the conscious and unconscious domains. Freud, "'Uncanny,'" 234. My thanks to Stephen Clingman for this reference.
7 Darnton, *Censors at Work*; McDonald, *Literature Police*; and Moore, "Introduction." See also Matteau, *Real and Imagined Readers*.
8 In "Surrealism and Pulp: The Limits of the Literary and Australian Customs," Nicole Moore discusses a case of Australian Customs censorship but looks fairly high up the bureaucratic chain, when the books in question had been passed to a specialist committee. Deana Heath has a chapter that touches on Australian Customs

censorship and looks much lower down the chain, producing a view that is more object oriented. Heath, *Purifying Empire*, chap. 4.

9. "Book Entitled De Dochter van dan Handsuffer [Hensopper]: Detention of," Attorney-General (AG) 1441, 4790, 1904, KAB, NASA, Cape Town.
10. "Complaint by Mr Speelman Regarding the Detention of Certain Books by the Customs," T 815, 1505, 1904–5.
11. "Resident Magistrate, Robertson. Books of a Political Nature Banned under Martial Law. Importation of Seditious Works by Messrs. J. Dusseau and Company," AG 1506, 10147, 1901–4.
12. Customs Management Act, 1872, clause 14, in Foster, Tennant, and Jackson, *Statutes of the Cape of Good Hope*.
13. Bickford-Smith, Van Heyningen, and Worden, *Cape Town*, 12–22.
14. "Resident Magistrate, Robertson. Books of a Political Nature Banned under Martial Law. Importation of Seditious Works by Messrs. J. Dusseau and Company," AG 1506, 10147, 1901–4.
15. "Detention of Book 'Vechten en Vluchten van Beyers en Kemp,'" T 912, 2145, 1905.
16. "Complaint by Mr Speelman Regarding the Detention of Certain Books by the Customs," T 815, 1505, 1904–5.
17. "Book Entitled De Dochter van dan Handsuffer [Hensopper]: Detention of," Cape Town, AG 1441, 4790, 1904.
18. "Customs and Excise. Prohibited Importation of Objectionable Goods (Section 23, Act 9/1913) Communist Literature," Secretary of the Treasury (TES) 3069, 12/351/4, 1923–33, SAB, NASA, Pretoria. (I have recorded the markings as they appear on the box. These do not accord with the online database, which records this file as TES 2884, F12/351/3.)
19. "Customs and Excise. Prohibited Importation of Objectionable Goods (Section 23, Act 9/1913) Communist Literature," TES 3069, 12/351/4, 1923–33.
20. Merrett, *Culture of Censorship*.
21. "Prohibited and Restricted Imports. Objectionable Literature," DEA 200, A10/6XA, 1941–46.
22. "Prohibited and Restricted Imports. Objectionable Literature," DEA 199, A10/6X, 1922.
23. "Customs Detention of Certain Books," Lieutenant-Governor (LTG) 19, 25/54, 1906, TAB, NASA, Pretoria.
24. "Duty Leviable on Pocket Books Containing Calenders on Inside Covers," DCU 86, 1540/06, 1906.
25. "Prohibited and Restricted Imports. Objectionable Literature," DEA 199, A 10/6X, 1952.
26. Khan, "When the Lion Feeds."
27. "Prohibited and Restricted Imports. Objectionable Literature," DEA 199, A10/6X, 1922.
28. "Prohibited and Restricted Imports. Objectionable Literature," DEA 199, A10/6X, 1922.

29 "Customs and Excise. Prohibited Importation of Objectionable Goods (Section 23, Act 9/1913) Communist Literature," TES 3069, 12/351/4, 1923–33.
30 "Prohibited and Restricted Imports. Objectionable Literature," DEA 200, A10/6XA, 1941–46.
31 "Customs and Excise. Prohibited Importation of Objectionable Goods (Section 23, Act 9/1913) Communist Literature," TES 3069, 12/351/4, 1923–33.
32 Davis, *Creating Postcolonial Literature*, 81–82.
33 "Prohibited and Restricted Imports. Objectionable Literature," DEA 200, A10/6X, 1946–50.
34 "Prohibited and Restricted Imports. Objectionable Literature," DEA 200, A10/6X, 1950–52.
35 "Prohibited and Restricted Imports. Objectionable Literature," DEA 200, A10/6X, 1946–50.
36 "Customs and Excise. Prohibited Importation of Objectionable Goods (Section 23, Act 9/1913) Communist Literature," TES 3069, 12/351/4, 1923–33.
37 "Customs and Excise. Prohibited Importation of Objectionable Goods (Section 23, Act 9/1913) Communist Literature," TES 3069, 12/351/4, 1923–33.
38 Heath, *Purifying Empire*, 140.
39 "Merchandise Marks Law," CKN 3/9, 128/6/4, 1910–36.
40 "Prohibited and Restricted Imports: Censorship," DEA 209, A10/26X, 1947.
41 "Customs and Excise. Prohibited Importation of Objectionable Goods (Section 23, Act 9/1913) Communist Literature," TES 3069, 12/351/4, 1923–33.
42 "Prohibited and Restricted Imports: Censorship," DEA 209, A10/26X, 1953.
43 "Prohibited and Restricted Imports: Censorship," DEA 209, A10/26X, 1953.
44 "Prohibited and Restricted Imports. Indecent and Objectionable Articles," DEA 200, A10/6X, 1952.
45 "Prohibited and Restricted Imports. Indecent and Objectionable Articles," DEA 199, A10/5X, 1939.
46 "Importation of Pirated Copyright Music," DCU 89, 1850/06, 1906.
47 "Prohibited and Restricted Imports. Objectionable Literature," DEA 199, A10/6X, 1922–38.
48 "Department of Interior. Censorship: 1) Entertainments (Censorship) Act 28/1931 and Amendments. 2) Board of Censors: Appointment and Remuneration of Members. 3) Board of Censors: Staff for," TES 696, F4/71, 1963.
49 McDonald, *Literature Police*.
50 Roberts, "South African Censorship," 43.
51 McDonald, *Literature Police*, 45–47.
52 The Literature Police: Literary Censorship in Apartheid South Africa, accessed December 5, 2019, https://theliteraturepolice.com/. These forms are drawn from the Interior Directorate of Publications (IDP) archive in NASA, Cape Town.
53 "Censors' Report on Coetzee's *Barbarians* 1980," The Literature Police, November 26, 1980, https://theliteraturepolice.files.wordpress.com/2018/07/censors-report-on-coetzees-barbarians-19802.pdf.

54 McDonald, *Literature Police*, 64. This trend is particularly clear in relation to the censorship of political writing, pamphlets, T-shirts, stickers, and the like. See "Objectional Object: 'Free Nelson Mandela,'" IDP 3/206, P87/6/123, 1987; "Objectionable Stamp: Fight to Free Our Leaders: The ANC Salutes Nelson Mandela," IDP 3/62, P78/II/1000, 1978; and "Objectionable Literature. Mary Benson. Nelson Mandela," IDP 3/101, P81/1/147, 1981–86.

CONCLUSION: DOCKSIDE GENRES AND POSTCOLONIAL LITERATURE

1 Duncan and Smyth, "Introductions," *Book Parts*, 4.
2 Deeds Registry Office, "Transcript of the Entries Registered in the Registry Book under Acts. No. 2 of 1873 and 4 of 1888 . . . Published in Terms of Section VI of the Last Mentioned Act," MSB729, 1894–1901.
3 Hofmeyr and Peterson, "Politics of the Page."
4 Newell, *Power to Name*; and Barber, "Authorship, Copyright and Quotation."
5 Chua et al., "Introduction."
6 Hofmeyr, *Gandhi's Printing Press*, 4.
7 New South Wales, Intelligence Department, *New South Wales*, 4.
8 Ingram, *Story of an African Seaport*, preface.
9 Ingram, *Colony of Natal*, 1.
10 Glenn, "Wreck of the *Grosvenor*."
11 Glenn, "Wreck of the *Grosvenor*."
12 Titlestad, *Shipwreck Narratives*.
13 Chapman, *Southern African Literature*, 1; and Gray, *Southern African Literature*, 116.
14 Samuelson, *Tidelines*.
15 Ingram, *Story of an African Seaport*, Table of Contents, vii.
16 Ingram, *Colony of Natal*, 83.
17 See Cathcart Methven's painting from 1906, reproduced in Terry Hutson, "A Sense of Déjà Vu," Ports and Ships: Shipping News—Reporting from the Harbours of South and Southern Africa, June 30, 2007, https://ports.co.za/shippingworld/article_2007_08_25_0917.html; for another painting and photograph see *Armadale Castle*, British and Commonwealth Register, accessed October 20, 2020, http://www.bandcstaffregister.com/page141.html (the untitled and undated painting appears under the heading "The Opening of Durban Bay to Larger Ships - 1904" and the photograph, also undated, is captioned "R.M.S. Armadale Castle, 12,973 Tons, Crossing the Durban Bar, Homeward Bound, on June 30, 1904"); for undated postcard see "SS Armadale Castle," Wikipedia, https://en.wikipedia.org/wiki/SS_Armadale_Castle#/media/File:RMS_Armadale_Castle.png (postcard entitled "R.M.S. 'Armadale Castle' 12973 Tons," also marked "Published by Sallo Epstein & Co., Durban").
18 Ingram, *Colony of Natal*, 83–84.
19 Ingram, *Colony of Natal*, "Contents of Sections," vi.
20 Mendelsohn, "Making the Urban Coast," 468.

21 Schreiner, *Story of an African Farm*, 74.
22 Schreiner, *Story of an African Farm*, 74–75.
23 Breckenridge, *Biometric State*, 5–6.
24 "COVID-19 and the Global Library Field," International Federation of Library Associations and Institutions, October 13, 2020, https://www.ifla.org/covid-19-and-libraries.

Bibliography

ARCHIVAL SOURCES: UNPUBLISHED GOVERNMENT DOCUMENTS

Attorney-General (AG), 1899-1923. Cape Archives Depot/Kaapse Argiefbewaarplek (KAB), National Archives of South Africa, Cape Town.

Attorney-General's Office (AGO), 1845-1928. Natal Archives Depot/Natalse Argiefbewaarplek (NAB), National Archives of South Africa, Pietermaritzburg.

Collector of Customs, Knysna (CKN), 1909-44. Cape Archives Depot/Kaapse Argiefbewaarplek (KAB), National Archives of South Africa, Cape Town.

Colonial Secretary's Office (CSO), 1842-1919. Natal Archives Depot/Natalse Argiefbewaarplek (NAB), National Archives of South Africa, Pietermaritzburg.

Customs and Excise (DEA), 1903-67. Central Archives Depot/Sentrale Argiefbewaarplek (SAB), National Archives of South Africa, Pretoria.

Director of Customs (DCU), 1900-1916. Transvaal Archives Depot/Transvaalse Argiefbewaarplek (TAB), National Archives of South Africa, Pretoria.

Governor-General, 1905-74. Central Archives Depot/Sentrale Argiefbewaarplek (SAB), National Archives of South Africa, Pretoria.

Governor of the Transvaal Colony, 1900-1916. Transvaal Archives Depot/Transvaalse Argiefbewaarplek (TAB), National Archives of South Africa, Pretoria.

Immigration Restriction Department, 1897-1912. Natal Archives Depot/Natalse Argiefbewaarplek (NAB), National Archives of South Africa, Pietermaritzburg.

Indian Immigration Department, 1858-1924. Natal Archives Depot/Natalse Argiefbewaarplek (NAB), National Archives of South Africa, Pietermaritzburg.

Interior Directorate of Publications (IDP), n.d. Cape Archives Depot/Kaapse Argiefbewaarplek (KAB), National Archives of South Africa, Cape Town.

Lieutenant-Governor, 1902-7. Transvaal Archives Depot/Transvaalse Argiefbewaarplek (TAB), National Archives of South Africa, Pretoria.

Minister of Justice and Public Works, 1861-1910. Natal Archives Depot/Natalse Argiefbewaarplek (NAB), National Archives of South Africa, Pietermaritzburg.

Natal Treasury, 1846–1912. Natal Archives Depot/Natalse Argiefbewaarplek (NAB), National Archives of South Africa, Pietermaritzburg.

Public Service Commission, 1912–73. Central Archives Depot/Sentrale Argiefbewaarplek (SAB), National Archives of South Africa, Pretoria.

Secretary for Foreign Affairs, 1899–1973. Central Archives Depot/Sentrale Argiefbewaarplek (SAB), National Archives of South Africa, Pretoria.

Secretary of Justice, 1899–1966. Central Archives Depot/Sentrale Argiefbewaarplek (SAB), National Archives of South Africa, Pretoria.

Secretary of Native Affairs (NTS), 1880–1975. Central Archives Depot/Sentrale Argiefbewaarplek (SAB), National Archives of South Africa, Pretoria.

Secretary of the Treasury (TES), 1904–74. Central Archives Depot/Sentrale Argiefbewaarplek (SAB), National Archives of South Africa, Pretoria.

Secretary to the Law Department (LD), 1900–1924. Transvaal Archives Depot/Transvaalse Argiefbewaarplek (TAB), National Archives of South Africa, Pretoria.

Trade Board, Cologne, 1947–72. Central Archives Depot/Sentrale Argiefbewaarplek (SAB), National Archives of South Africa, Pretoria.

Treasury Department (T), 1904–12. Cape Archives Depot/Kaapse Argiefbewaarplek (KAB), National Archives of South Africa, Cape Town.

PUBLISHED SOURCES

Adderley, Rosanne Marion. *"New Negroes from Africa": Slave Trade Abolition and Free African Settlement in the Nineteenth-Century Caribbean*. Bloomington: Indiana University Press, 2006.

Adelaide Intelligence and Tourist Bureau, comp. *South Australia: Handbook of Information for Settlers, Tourists and Others*. Adelaide: R. E. E. Rogers, 1913.

Agius, Dionisius A. "Red Sea Folk Beliefs: A Maritime Spirit Landscape." *Northeast African Studies* 17, no. 1 (2017): 131–61.

Alaimo, Stacy. "Violet-Black." In *Prismatic Ecology: Ecotheory beyond Green*, edited by Jeffrey Jerome Cohen, 233–51. Minneapolis: University of Minnesota Press, 2013.

Allen, Nicholas, Nick Groom, and Jos Smith, eds. *Coastal Works: Cultures of the Atlantic Edge*. Oxford: Oxford University Press, 2017.

Allewaert, Monique. "Super Fly: François Makandal's Colonial Semiotics." *American Literature* 91, no. 3 (2019): 459–90.

Asakura, Hironori. *World History of the Customs and Tariff*. Brussels: World Customs Organization, 2003.

Ashworth, William. *Customs and Excise: Trade, Production and Consumption in England, 1640–1845*. Oxford: Oxford University Press, 2003. Kindle.

Atton, Henry, and Henry Hurst Holland. *The King's Customs*. Vol. 2. London: John Murray, 1910.

Baderoon, Gabeba. "The African Oceans: Tracing the Sea as Memory of Slavery in South African Literature and Culture." *Research in African Literatures* 40, no. 4 (2009): 89–107.

Banerjee, Sukanya. *Becoming Imperial Citizens: Indians in the Late-Victorian Empire*. Durham, NC: Duke University Press, 2010.

Barber, Karin. "Authorship, Copyright and Quotation in Oral and Print Spheres in Early Colonial Yorubaland." In *Copyright Africa: How Intellectual Property, Media and Markets Transform Immaterial Cultural Goods*, edited by Ute Röschenthaler and Mamadou Diawara, 105-27. Oxford: Sean Kingston, 2016.

Barnes, David S. "Cargo, 'Infection,' and the Logic of Quarantine in the Nineteenth Century." *Bulletin of the History of Medicine* 88, no. 1 (2014): 75-101.

Bashford, Alison. "Maritime Quarantine: Linking Old World and New World Histories." In *Quarantine: Local and Global Histories*, edited by Alison Bashford, 1-12. London: Palgrave, 2016.

Basson, S. P. "Regte op invoere as instrument van die ekonomiese politiek: 'N historiese en analitiese beskouing." PhD diss., University of Pretoria, 1988.

Behar, Katherine. "An Introduction to OOF." In *Object-Oriented Feminism*, edited by Katherine Behar, locs. 46-773 of 5242. Minneapolis: University of Minnesota Press, 2016. Kindle.

Bell, Currer [Charlotte Brontë]. *Villette*. 1853. London: Smith, Elder, 1889.

Bender, Colin. *Who Saved Natal? The Story of the Victorian Harbour Engineers of Colonial Port Natal*. Durban: n.p., 1988.

Bengal, Customs Department. *The Calcutta Customs Calculation Manual, etc.* Calcutta: Bengal Customs Department, 1922.

Bennett, Jane. "Systems and Things: A Response to Graham Harman and Timothy Morton." *New Literary History* 43, no. 2 (2012): 225-33.

Bennett, Jane. *Vibrant Matter: A Political Ecology of Things*. Durham, NC: Duke University Press, 2010.

Bennett, Joshua. "Beyond the Vomiting Dark." In *Ecopoetics: Essays in the Field*, edited by Angela Hume and Gillian Osborne, 102-17. Iowa City: University of Iowa Press, 2018.

Bently, Lionel. "Copyright, Translations, and Relations between Britain and India in the Nineteenth and Early Twentieth Centuries." *Chicago-Kent Law Review* 82, no. 3 (2007): 1181-240.

Bently, Lionel. "The 'Extraordinary Multiplicity' of Intellectual Property Laws in the British Colonies in the Nineteenth Century." *Theoretical Inquiries in Law* 12, no. 1 (2011): 161-200. https://philpapers.org/rec/BENTEM-3.

Bergemann, Karl J. "Council of (In)Justice: Crime, Status, Punishment and the Decision-Makers in the 1730s Cape Justice System." Master's thesis, University of Cape Town, 2011.

Bergvall, Caroline. *Drift*. New York: Nightboat Books, 2014.

Bernard, Penelope Susan. "Messages from the Deep: Water Divinities, Dreams and Diviners in Southern Africa." PhD diss., Rhodes University, 2010.

Best, Stephen M. *The Fugitive's Properties: Law and the Poetics of Possession*. Chicago: University of Chicago Press, 2004. Kindle.

Bickford-Smith, Vivian, Elizabeth van Heyningen, and Nigel Worden. *Cape Town in the Twentieth Century: An Illustrated Social History*. Cape Town: David Philip, 1999.

Birnhack, Michael D. *Colonial Copyright: Intellectual Property in Mandate Palestine*. Oxford: Oxford University Press, 2012.

Blum, Hester. *The View from the Mast-Head: Maritime Imagination and Antebellum American Sea Narratives*. Chapel Hill: University of North Carolina Press, 2008.

Bogost, Ian. *Alien Phenomenology, or What It's Like to Be a Thing*. Minneapolis: University of Minnesota Press, 2012.

Bracha, Oren. "The Ideology of Authorship Revisited: Authors, Markets, and Liberal Values in Early American Copyright." *Yale Law Review* 118, no. 2 (2008): 186–271.

Breckenridge, Keith. *The Biometric State: The Global Politics of Identification and Surveillance in South Africa, 1850 to the Present*. Cambridge: Cambridge University Press, 2014.

Bruwer, A. J. *Protection in South Africa*. Stellenbosch: Pro Ecclesia, 1923.

Callebert, Ralph Frans. "Livelihood Strategies of Dock Workers in Durban, c. 1900–1959." PhD diss., Queen's University, Kingston, 2011.

Carroll, Siobhan. *An Empire of Air and Water: Uncolonizable Space in the British Imagination, 1750–1850*. Philadelphia: University of Pennsylvania Press, 2015.

Carson, Edward A. "The Customs Plantation Records." *Journal of the Society of Archivists* 4, no. 3 (1971): 212–21.

Chalfin, Brenda. *Neoliberal Frontiers: An Ethnography of Sovereignty in West Africa*. Chicago: University of Chicago Press, 2010.

Chan, Suzanna. "'Alive . . . Again': Unmoored in the Aquafuture of Ellen Gallagher's 'Watery Ecstatic.'" *Women's Studies Quarterly* 45, no. 1/2 (2017): 246–63.

Chapman, Michael. *Southern African Literature*. London: Longman, 1996.

Chua, Charmaine, Martin Danyluk, Deborah Cowen, and Laleh Khalili. "Introduction: Turbulent Circulation: Building a Critical Engagement with Logistics." *Environment and Planning D: Society and Space* 36, no. 4 (2018): 617–29.

Clements, George. *Clements' Customs Pocket Manual, etc*. London: Smith and Elder and T. Ostell, 1842.

Clements, George. *Customs Guide*. London: n.p., 1835.

Cloete, Stuart. *Turning Wheels*. London: Collins, 1937.

Coetzee, J. M. "Farm Novel and *Plaasroman*." In *White Writing: On the Culture of Letters in South Africa*, 65–84. 1988. Johannesburg: Pentz, 2017.

Coghlan, Robert Nesbit. *Customs Manual*. Karachi: Commissioner's Press, 1884.

Cohen, Jeffrey Jerome, and Lowell Duckert, eds. *Elemental Ecocriticism: Thinking with Earth, Air, Water, and Fire*. Minneapolis: University of Minnesota Press, 2015.

Cohen, Margaret. "The Chronotopes of the Sea." In *The Novel*, vol. 2, *Forms and Themes*, edited by Franco Moretti, 647–66. Princeton, NJ: Princeton University Press, 2007.

Cohen, Margaret. *The Novel and the Sea*. Princeton, NJ: Princeton University Press, 2010.

Cohen, Margaret. "Seeing through Water: The Paintings of Zarh Pritchard." In *Coastal Works: Cultures of the Atlantic Edge*, edited by Nicholas Allen, Nick Groom, and Jos Smith, 205–24. Oxford: Oxford University Press, 2017.

Cohen, Margaret. "The Shipwreck as Undersea Gothic." In *The Aesthetics of the Undersea*, edited by Margaret Cohen and Killian Quigley, 155–65. Abingdon, UK: Routledge, 2019.

Cohen, Margaret. "The Underwater Imagination: From Environment to Film Set, 1954-1956." *English Language Notes* 57, no. 1 (2019): 51-71.

Colesky, Theo. "A Comparative Study of Customs Tariff Classification." PhD diss., University of Pretoria, 2014.

Collen, Lindsey. *Mutiny*. London: Bloomsbury, 2001.

Colony of Natal, Natal Harbour Department. *Regulations of the Port and Harbour of Port Natal*. Pietermaritzburg: P. Davis, 1905.

Conrad, Joseph. *The Mirror of the Sea*. New York: Harpers, 1906.

Cooper, Frederick. *Africa since 1940: The Past of the Present*. Cambridge: Cambridge University Press, 2002.

Crain, Patricia. *The Story of A: The Alphabetization of America from* The New England Primer *to* The Scarlet Letter. Stanford, CA: Stanford University Press, 2002.

da Cunha, Dilip. *The Invention of Rivers: Alexander's Eye and Ganga's Descent*. Philadelphia: University of Pennsylvania Press, 2018.

da Cunha, Dilip, and Anuradha Mathur. *Soak: Mumbai in an Estuary*. Delhi: Rupa, 2009.

Dalbello, Marija. "Reading Immigrants: Immigration of Site and Process of Reading and Writing." In *Reading and Writing from Below: Exploring the Margins of Modernity*, edited by Ann-Catrine Edlund, T. G. Ashplant, and Anna Kuismin, 169-96. Umeå: Umeå University and the Royal Skyttean Society, 2016.

Darnton, Robert. *Censors at Work: How States Shaped Literature*. New York: W. W. Norton, 2014.

Da Silva, Daniel Domingues, David Eltis, Philip Misevich, and Olatunji Ojo. "The Diaspora of Africans Liberated from Slave Ships in the Nineteenth Century." *Journal of African History* 55, no. 3 (2014): 347-69.

Davis, Caroline. *Creating Postcolonial Literature: African Writers and British Publishers*. Basingstoke, UK: Palgrave Macmillan, 2013.

Dean, Owen H. "The Application of the Copyright Act, 1978, to Works Made Prior to 1979." PhD diss., University of Stellenbosch, 1988.

Dean, Owen H. *The Summit Syndrome*. Bloomington, IN: AuthorHouse, 2017.

Deckard, Sharae. "The Political Ecology of Storms in Caribbean Literature." In *The Caribbean: Aesthetics, World-Ecology, Politics*, edited by Chris Campbell and Michael Niblett, 25-45. Liverpool: Liverpool University Press, 2016.

De Kock, M. H. *Selected Subjects in the Economic History of South Africa*. Cape Town: Juta, 1924.

Delmas, Adrien. "From Travelling to History: An Outline of the VOC Writing System during the 17th Century." In *Written Culture in a Colonial Context: Africa and the Americas, 1500-1900*, edited by Adrien Delmas and Nigel Penn, 99-126. Leiden: Brill, 2012.

DeLoughrey, Elizabeth. "Submarine Futures of the Anthropocene." *Comparative Literature* 69, no. 1 (2017): 32-44.

DeLoughrey, Elizabeth. "Toward a Critical Ocean Studies for the Anthropocene." *English Language Notes* 57, no. 1 (2019): 21-36.

Department of Commercial Intelligence and Statistics, India. *Indian Customs Tariff*. Delhi: Manager of Publications, 1935.

de Prada-Samper, José Manuel. "'A Partial Clue': The Genesis and Context of Qing and Orpen's Conversation." In *On the Trail of Qing and Orpen*, edited by José Manuel de Prada-Samper, Menan du Plessis, Jeremy Hollman, Jill Weintroub, Justine Wintjes, and John Wright, 29-96. Johannesburg: Standard Bank of South Africa, 2016.

Desai, Ashwin, and Goolam Vahed. *Inside Indian Indenture: A South African Story*. Cape Town: HSRC Press, 2010.

Dhupelia-Mesthrie, Uma. "False Fathers and False Sons: Immigration Officials in Cape Town, Documents and Verifying Minor Sons from India in the First Half of the Twentieth Century." *Kronos* 40, no. 1 (2014): 99-132.

Dickens, Charles. *Great Expectations*. 1861. Oxford: Clarendon Press, 1993.

Dietrich, Eric. "Algorithm." In *The MIT Encyclopedia on the Cognitive Sciences*, edited by Robert Andrew Will and Frank C. Keil, 11. Cambridge, MA: MIT Press, 2001.

"Die Djin-Vrou" (The Djinn Woman). In *Uit die Slamse Buurt: Deel 1: Kaapse Sprokies, Fabels en Legendes*, retold by I. D. du Plessis, 75-78. Cape Town: Nasionale Pers, 1939.

Duguid, Paul. "Information in the Mark and the Marketplace: A Multivocal Approach." *Enterprise and Society* 15, no. 1 (2014): 19-21.

Duncan, Dennis. "Indexes." In *Book Parts*, edited by Dennis Duncan and Adam Smyth, 265-74. Oxford: Oxford University Press, 2019.

Duncan, Dennis, and Adam Smyth. "Introductions." In *Book Parts*, edited by Dennis Duncan and Adam Smyth, 1-10. Oxford: Oxford University Press, 2019.

Duszat, Michael. "Foucault's Laughter: Enumeration, Rewriting, and the Construction of the Essayist in Borges's 'The Analytical Language of John Wilkins.'" *Orbis Litterarum* 67, no. 3 (2012): 193-218.

Elias, Ann. *The Coral Empire: Underwater Oceans, Colonial Tropics, Visual Modernity*. Durham, NC: Duke University Press, 2019.

Ellis, Beverley. "The Impact of White Settlers on the Natural Environment of Natal, 1845-1870." In *South Africa's Environmental History: Cases and Comparisons*, edited by Stephen Dovers, Ruth Edgecombe, and Bill Guest, 34-47. Pietermaritzburg: University of Natal Press, 1985.

Engelmann, Lukas, and Christos Lynteris. *Sulphuric Utopias: A History of Maritime Fumigation*. Cambridge, MA: MIT Press, 2020.

Engelmann, Sasha. "Towards a Poetics of Air: Sequencing and Surfacing Breath." *Transactions of the Institute of British Geographers* 40, no. 3 (2015): 430-44.

Ette, Ottmar. "Khal Torabully: 'Coolies' and Corals, or Living in Transarchipelagic Worlds." *Journal of the African Literature Association* 11, no. 1 (2017): 112-19.

Finney, Nikky. "Shark Bite." In *The World Is Round*, 56-58. Chicago: Northwestern University Press, 2013.

Finney, Nikky. "The Undersea World of Jacques Cousteau." In *The World Is Round*, 31-37. Chicago: Northwestern University Press, 2013.

Fletcher, Anne. *The London Custom House: Souvenir Guidebook*. London: London Custom House, 2000.

Fontein, Joost. "The Power of Water: Landscape, Water and the State in Southern and

Eastern Africa: An Introduction." *Journal of Southern African Studies* 34, no. 4 (2008): 737–56.

Foster, Joseph, Hercules Tennant, and E. M. Jackson, eds. *Statutes of the Cape of Good Hope, 1652–1886*. Cape Town: W. A. Richards and Son, 1887.

Foucault, Michel. *The Order of Things: An Archeology of the Human Sciences*. 1970. London: Routledge, 2002.

Freud, Sigmund. "The 'Uncanny.'" In *The Standard Edition of the Complete Psychological Works of Sigmund Freud*, edited by James Strachey, 17:219–52. London: Hogarth, 1955.

Gandhi, Mahatma. *Collected Works of Mahatma Gandhi*. Vol. 2. New Delhi: Publications Division, Government of India, 1999. http://www.gandhiashramsevagram.org/gandhi-literature/mahatma-gandhi-collected-works-volume-2.pdf.

General Instructions for the Landing-Waiters and King's-Waiters, in the Port of London. N.p.: n.p., 1805.

Ghosh, Amitav. *The Hungry Tide*. New Delhi: Penguin, 2004.

Ghosh, Amitav. *In an Antique Land: History in the Guise of a Traveler's Tale*. London: Vintage, 1992.

Ghosh, Amitav. *River of Smoke*. New York: Picador, 2011.

Ghosh, Amitav. *Sea of Poppies*. New York: Picador, 2008.

Gillis, John R. *The Human Shore: Seacoasts in History*. Chicago: University of Chicago Press, 2012.

Gitelman, Lisa. "Not." In *Further Reading*, edited by Matthew Rubery and Leah Price. Oxford: Oxford University Press, 2020. https://doi.org/10.1093/oxfordhb/9780198809791.013.31.

Gitelman, Lisa. *Paper Knowledge: Toward a Media History of Documents*. Durham, NC: Duke University Press, 2012.

Glenn, Ian E. "The Wreck of the *Grosvenor* and the Making of South African Literature." *English in Africa* 22, no. 2 (1995): 1–18.

Gordimer, Nadine. "Censorship and the Artist." *Staffrider* 7, no. 2 (1988): 11–16.

Graber, Darin Trent. "Flow Dynamics in Nineteenth-Century British Literature and Culture." PhD diss., University of Colorado, 2017.

Graeber, David. *The Utopia of Rules: On Technology, Stupidity, and the Secret Joys of Bureaucracy*. Brooklyn, NY: Melville House, 2016.

Gray, Stephen. *Southern African Literature: An Introduction*. New York: Barnes and Noble, 1979.

The Greater Dictionary of isiXhosa. Alice, South Africa: University of Fort Hare, 2006.

Gregory, T. E. *Tariffs: A Study of Method*. London: Griffin, 1921.

Gurnah, Abdulrazak. *By the Sea*. London: Bloomsbury, 2002.

Guzmán, Patricio. *The Pearl Button*. N.p.: Kino Lorber Edu, 2017. Video.

Hardy, Thomas. "The Distracted Preacher." In *The Distracted Preacher and Other Tales*, 40–98. 1879. London: Penguin, 1986.

Harman, Graham. *Tool-Being: Heidegger and the Metaphysics of Objects*. Peru, IL: Open Court, 2002.

Harney, Stefano, and Fred Moten. *The Undercommons: Fugitive Planning and Black Study*. Wivenhoe: Minor Compositions, 2013.

Harris, Cheryl I. "Whiteness as Property." *Harvard Law Review* 106, no. 8 (1993): 1707–91.

Hawthorne, Nathaniel. *The Scarlet Letter*. 1850. Philadelphia: Henry Altemus, 1892.

Hayward, Eva. "More Lessons from a Starfish: Prefixial Flesh and Transspeciated Selves." *Women's Studies Quarterly* 36, no. 3/4 (2008): 64–85.

Heath, Deana. *Purifying Empire: Obscenity and the Politics of Moral Regulation in Britain, India and Australia*. Cambridge: Cambridge University Press, 2010.

Hein, Carola. "Port Cities." In *The Oxford Handbook of Cities in World History*, edited by Peter Clark, 809–27. Oxford: Oxford University Press, 2013.

Hensley, Nathan K., and Philip Steer. "Ecological Formalism: or, Love among the Ruins." In *Ecological Form: System and Aesthetics in the Age of Empire*, edited by Nathan K. Hensley and Philip Steer, 1–14. New York: Fordham University Press, 2018.

Heydenrych, Lucille. "Port Natal Harbour, c. 1850–1897." In *Enterprise and Exploitation in a Victorian Colony: Aspects of the Economic and Social History of Colonial Natal*, edited by Bill Guest and John M. Sellers, 17–45. Pietermaritzburg: University of Natal Press, 1985.

Higginson, John Hedley. *Tariffs at Work: An Outline of Practical Tariff Administration, with Special Reference to the United States and Canada*. London: P. S. King, 1913.

Hoag, Colin, and Matthew S. Hull. *A Review of the Anthropological Literature on the Civil Service*. Washington, DC: World Bank, 2017.

Hofmeyr, Isabel. "Colonial Copyright and Port Cities: Material Histories and Intellectual Property." *Comparative Literature* 70, no. 3 (2018): 264–77.

Hofmeyr, Isabel. *Gandhi's Printing Press: Experiments in Slow Reading*. Cambridge, MA: Harvard University Press, 2013.

Hofmeyr, Isabel. "Imperialism above and below the Water Line: Making Space Up (and Down) in a Colonial Port City." *Interventions* 22, no. 8 (2020): 1032–44.

Hofmeyr, Isabel. "In the Custom House." In *Further Reading*, edited by Matthew Rubery and Leah Price. Oxford: Oxford University Press, 2020. https://doi.org/10.1093/oxfordhb/9780198809791.013.3.

Hofmeyr, Isabel. *The Portable Bunyan: A Transnational History of* The Pilgrim's Progress. Princeton, NJ: Princeton University Press, 2004.

Hofmeyr, Isabel. "Provisional Notes on Hydrocolonialism." *English Language Notes* 57, no. 1 (2019): 11–20.

Hofmeyr, Isabel, and Kerry Bystrom. "Oceanic Routes: Post-It Notes on Hydrocolonialism." *Comparative Literature* 69, no. 1 (2017): 1–6.

Hofmeyr, Isabel, and Derek Peterson. "The Politics of the Page: Cutting and Pasting in South African and African-American Newspapers." *Social Dynamics* 45, no. 1 (2019): 1–25.

Hsiung, Hansun. "Knowledge Made Cheap: Global Learners and the Logistics of Reading." *PMLA* 134, no. 1 (2019): 137–43.

Hughes, David McDermott. "Hydrology of Hope: Farm Dams, Conservation, and Whiteness in Zimbabwe." *American Ethnologist* 33, no. 2 (2006): 269–87.

Hull, Matthew S. *Government of Paper: The Materiality of Bureaucracy in Urban Pakistan.* Berkeley: University of California Press, 2012.

Hyslop, Jonathan. "Guns, Drugs and Revolutionary Propaganda: Indian Sailors and Smuggling in the 1920s." *South African Historical Journal* 61, no. 4 (2009): 838–46.

Hyslop, Jonathan. "'Undesirable Inhabitants of the Union . . . Supplying Liquor to Natives': D. F. Malan and the Deportation of South Africa's British and Irish Lumpen Proletarians, 1924–1933." *Kronos* 40, no. 1 (2014): 178–97.

Ingram, J. Forsyth. *Colony of Natal: Official Illustrated Handbook and Railway Guide.* London: Causton and Sons, 1895.

Ingram, J. Forsyth. *The Story of an African Seaport: Being the History of the Port and Borough of Durban, the Seaport of Natal.* Durban: G. Coester, 1899.

Instructions to Preventive Men. London: Darling, 1909.

Irr, Caren. *Pink Pirates: Contemporary American Women Writers and Copyright.* Iowa City: University of Iowa Press, 2010.

Issur, Kumari. "Postcolonial Narratives of the Tropical Cyclone in the Indian Ocean." Paper presented at the workshop Literary Ecologies of the Indian Ocean World: Mauritian and Southern African Intersections, University of the Witwatersrand, Johannesburg, August 16–17, 2018.

Jaszi, Peter. "Towards a Theory of Copyright: The Metamorphoses of 'Authorship.'" *Duke Law Journal* 1991, no. 2 (1991): 455–502.

Johns, Adrian. *The Nature of the Book: Print and Knowledge in the Making.* Chicago: University of Chicago Press, 1998.

Jones, Darryl. "'As If the Water Had but Newly Retired from the Face of the Earth': The Flood in Victorian Fiction." *Literature and Theology* 26, no. 4 (2012): 439–58.

Jue, Melody. "Submerging Kittler." *Social Science Information* 57, no. 3 (2018): 476–82.

Jue, Melody. *Wild Blue Media: Thinking through Seawater.* Durham, NC: Duke University Press, 2020.

Jue, Melody Christina. "Wild Blue Media: Thinking through Seawater." PhD diss., Duke University, 2015.

Kerly, Duncan Mackenzie, and F. G. Underday. *The Law of Trade-Marks, Trade-Name, and Merchandise Marks with Chapters on Trade Secret and Trade Libel, and a Full Collection of Statues, Rules, Forms and Precedents.* London: Sweet and Maxwell, 1901.

Khan, Ellison. "When the Lion Feeds—and the Censor Pounces: A Disquisition on the Banning of Immoral Publications in South Africa." *South African Law Journal* 88 (1966): 278–336.

Killingray, David. "Introduction: Imperial Seas: Cultural Exchange and Commerce in the British Empire, 1780–1900." In *Maritime Empires: British Imperial Maritime Trade in the Nineteenth Century*, edited by David Killingray, Margarette Lincoln, and Nigel Rigby, 1–12. Woodbridge, UK: Boydell and National Maritime Museum, 2004.

Kraut, Anthea. *Choreographing Copyright: Race, Gender, and Intellectual Property Rights in American Dance.* New York: Oxford University Press, 2016.

Lake, Marilyn, and Henry Reynolds. *Drawing the Global Colour Line: White Men's Countries and the International Challenge of Racial Equality*. Cambridge: Cambridge University Press, 2008.

Lan, David. *Guns and Rain: Guerrillas and Spirit Mediums in Zimbabwe*. London: James Currey, 1985.

Lavery, Charne. "Writing the Indian Ocean in Selected Fiction by Joseph Conrad, Amitav Ghosh, Abdulrazak Gurnah and Lindsey Collen." PhD diss., Oxford University, 2013.

Lewis, Alfred J. S. *The South African Customs Union Tariff*. Cape Town: W. A. Richards, 1902.

Liebich, Susann. "Connected Readers: Reading Practices and Communities across the British Empire, c. 1890–1930." PhD diss., Victoria University of Wellington, 2012.

Linton, Jamie, and Jessica Budds. "The Hydrosocial Cycle: Defining and Mobilizing a Relational-Dialectical Approach to Water." *Geoforum* 57 (2014): 170–80.

MacDonald, Andrew. "The Identity Thieves of the Indian Ocean: Forgery, Fraud and the Origins of South African Immigration Control, 1890s–1920s." In *Recognition and Registration: Documenting the Person in World History*, edited by Keith Breckenridge and Simon Szreter, 390–428. Oxford: Oxford University Press, 2012.

MacDonald, Andrew. "Strangers in a Strange Land: Undesirables and Border-Controls in Colonial Durban, 1987–c.1910." Master's thesis, University of KwaZulu-Natal, 2007.

Martel, Yann. *The Life of Pi*. Edinburgh: Canongate, 2003.

Martens, Jeremy. "Pioneering the Dictation Test? The Creation and Administration of Western Australia's Immigration Restriction Act, 1897–1901." *Studies in Western Australian History* 28 (2013): 47–67.

Matsha, Rachel Matteau. *Real and Imagined Readers: Censorship, Publishing and Reading under Apartheid*. Pietermaritzburg: University of KwaZulu-Natal Press, 2019.

Mawani, Renisa. *Across Oceans of Law: The* Komagata Maru *and Jurisdiction in the Time of Empire*. Durham, NC: Duke University Press, 2018.

Maynard, John. "'In the Interests of Our People': The Influence of Garveyism on the Rise of Australian Aboriginal Political Activism." *Aboriginal History* 29 (2005): 1–22.

McCormack, Derek P. *Atmospheric Things: On the Allure of Elemental Envelopment*. Durham, NC: Duke University Press, 2018.

McDonald, Peter D. *The Literature Police: Apartheid Censorship and Its Cultural Consequences*. Oxford: Oxford University Press, 2009.

McGill, Meredith L. *American Literature and the Culture of Reprinting, 1834–1853*. Philadelphia: University of Pennsylvania Press, 2003.

McGill, Meredith L. "Copyright." In *A History of the Book in America*, vol. 2, *An Extensive Republic: Print, Culture, and Society in the New Nation, 1790–1840*, edited by Robert A. Gross and Mary Kelley, 198–211. Chapel Hill: University of North Carolina Press, 2010.

McGill, Meredith L. "Copyright and Intellectual Property: The State of the Discipline." *Book History* 16, no. 1 (2013): 387–427.

McGuire, E. B. *The British Tariff System*. 1939. London: Methuen, 1951.

McKenzie, Kirsten. "The Daemon behind the Curtain: William Edwards and the Theatre of Liberty." *South African Journal of History* 61, no. 3 (2009): 482–504.

McKittrick, Meredith. "Making Rain, Making Maps: Competing Geographies of Water and Power in Southwestern Africa." *Journal of African History* 58, no. 2 (2017): 187-212.

Melville, Herman. *Moby Dick, or The Whale*. 1851. London: Constable, 1922.

Mendelsohn, Ben. "Making the Urban Coast: A Geosocial Reading of Land, Sand, and Water in Lagos, Nigeria." *Comparative Studies of South Asia, Africa and the Middle East* 38, no. 3 (2018): 455-72.

Merrett, Christopher. *A Culture of Censorship: Secrecy and Intellectual Repression in South Africa*. Cape Town: David Philip, 1994.

Minchinton, Walter E. "E. E. Williams: 'Made in Germany' and After." *Vierteljahrschrift für Sozial- und Wirtschaftsgeschichte* 62, no. 2 (1975): 229-42.

Mohulatsi, Mapule. "Black Aesthetics and the Deep Ocean." Master's thesis, University of the Witwatersrand, 2019.

Moore, Nicole. "Introduction." In *Censorship and the Limits of the Literary: A Global View*, edited by Nicole Moore, 1-10. London: Bloomsbury, 2015.

Moore, Nicole. "Surrealism and Pulp: The Limits of the Literary and Australian Customs." In *Censorship and the Limits of the Literary: A Global View*, edited by Nicole Moore, 105-18. London: Bloomsbury, 2015.

Morshead, L. F., comp. *The Merchandise Marks Manual*. Calcutta: Government Printer, 1910.

Mosse, David. *The Rule of Water: Statecraft, Ecology and Collective Action in South India*. New Delhi: Oxford University Press, 2003.

Mukhopadhyay, Priyasha. "On Not Reading *The Soldier's Pocket-Book for Field Service*." *Journal of Victorian Culture* 22, no. 1 (2017): 40-56.

Natal (Colony), Commission on the Port and Harbour of Natal. *Report and Second Interim Report*. Pietermaritzburg: Colonial Secretary's Office, 1880.

Newell, Stephanie. *The Power to Name: A History of Anonymity in West Africa*. Athens: Ohio University Press, 2013.

New South Wales, Intelligence Department. *New South Wales, the Mother State of Australia: A Guide for Immigrants and Settlers*. Sydney: New South Wales, Intelligence Department, 1906.

Nuttall, Sarah. "Pluvial Time/Wet Form." *New Literary History* 51, no. 2 (2020): 455-72.

Okorafor, Nnedi. *Lagoon*. New York: Saga, 2016.

Opland, Jeff. *Xhosa Poets and Poetry*. Cape Town: David Philip, 1998.

Oram, R. B. *Cargo Handling and the Modern Port City*. London: Pergamon, 1964.

Orenstein, Dara. "Warehouses on Wheels." *Environment and Planning D: Society and Space* 36, no. 4 (2018): 648-65.

Payn, Howard. *The Merchandise Marks Act of 1887: With Special Reference to the Importation Sections and the Customs Regulations and Orders Made Thereunder Together with the Conventions with Foreign States for Protection of Trade Marks and Orders in Council under the Patents, Designs and Trade Marks Act, 1883, etc*. London: Stevens and Sons, 1888.

Pearson, Michael. *The Indian Ocean*. London: Routledge, 2008.

Peires, Jeffrey. "Lovedale Press: Literature for the Bantu Revisited." *English in Africa* 71, no. 1 (1980): 71-85.

Peters, John Durham. *The Marvelous Clouds: Toward a Philosophy of Elemental Media.* Chicago: University of Chicago Press, 2015.
Pettitt, Clare. *Patent Inventions: Intellectual Property and the Victorian Novel.* Oxford: Oxford University Press, 2004.
Peukert, Alexander. "The Colonial Legacy of the International Copyright System." In *Copyright Africa: How Intellectual Property, Media and Markets Transform Immaterial Cultural Goods*, edited by Ute Röschenthaler and Mamadou Diawara, 37–68. Oxford: Sean Kingston, 2016.
Philip, M. NourbeSe. *Zong!* Middletown, CT: Wesleyan University Press, 2008.
Posmentier, Sonya. *Cultivation and Catastrophe: The Lyric Ecology of Modern Black Literature.* Baltimore: Johns Hopkins University Press, 2017.
Price, Leah. *How to Do Things with Books in Victorian Britain.* Princeton, NJ: Princeton University Press, 2012.
Pritchard, Sara B. "From Hydroimperialism to Hydrocapitalism: 'French' Hydraulics in France, North Africa, and Beyond." *Social Studies in Science* 42, no. 4 (2012): 591–615.
Putuma, Koleka. *Collective Amnesia.* Cape Town: uHlanga, 2017.
Quigley, Killian. "The Porcellaneous Ocean: Matter and Meaning in the Rococo Undersea." In *The Aesthetics of the Undersea*, edited by Margaret Cohen and Killian Quigley, 28–41. Abingdon, UK: Routledge, 2019.
Rajagopal, Arvind. "Early Publicity in India: Trademark, Branding and Advertisement." *Marg: A Magazine of the Arts* 68, no. 3 (2017): 88–99.
Rao, Gautham. *National Duties: Custom Houses and the Making of the American State.* Chicago: University of Chicago Press, 2016.
Rideout, Eric Hardwicke. *The Custom House: Liverpool.* Liverpool: William C. Elly, 1928.
Roberts, Sheila. "South African Censorship and the Case of *Burger's Daughter.*" *Journal of Postcolonial Writing* 20, no. 1 (1981): 41–48.
Robins, Joseph. *Custom House People.* Dublin: Institute of Public Administration, 1993.
Rose, Mark. *Authors and Owners: The Invention of Copyright.* Cambridge, MA: Harvard University Press, 1995.
Rubusana, W. B. *Zemk'inkomo magwalandini.* 1906. Frome: Burton and Tanner, 1911.
Rudy, Jason R. *Imagined Homelands: British Poetry in the Colonies.* Baltimore: Johns Hopkins University Press, 2017.
Rukavina, Alison. *The Development of the International Book Trade, 1870–1895.* Basingstoke, UK: Palgrave Macmillan, 2010.
Saint-Amour, Paul K. *The Copywrights: Intellectual Property and the Literary Imagination.* Ithaca, NY: Cornell University Press, 2003.
Samuelson, Meg. "Coastal Form: Amphibian Positions, Wider Worlds and Planetary Horizons on the African Indian Ocean Littoral." *Comparative Literature* 69, no. 1 (2017): 16–24.
Samuelson, Meg. *Tidelines: Sea and Shore in South African Literature.* London: Palgrave, forthcoming.
Sato, Shohei. "'Operation Legacy': Britain's Destruction and Concealment of Colonial

Records Worldwide." *Journal of Imperial and Commonwealth History* 45, no. 4 (2017): 697–719.

Saunders, David. "Copyright, Obscenity and Literary History." *ELH* 57, no. 2 (1990): 431–44.

Sayer, Henry. *The Homeward-Bound Passenger's Companion, via the Cape: Compiled for the Use of Residents in India, and the British Possessions Adjacent Thereto; with a Tariff of Customs Duties*. [London]: C. Beckett, 1849.

Scardamaglia, Amanda. "The Colonial Trade Mark Regime: Parallel Rationales, Theories and Frameworks." *King's Law Journal* 22, no. 3 (2011): 259–88.

Schmidt, Michael. *Death Flight: Apartheid's Secret Doctrine of Disappearance*. Cape Town: Tafelberg, 2020.

Schreiner, Olive [Ralph Iron]. *The Story of an African Farm*. 1883. Digireads.com, 2002.

Searchy, Arthur, comp. *The Custom House Handbook*. Adelaide: Government Printer, 1889.

Serpell, Namwali. *The Old Drift*. London: Hogarth, 2019.

Seville, Catherine. *The Internationalisation of Copyright Law: Books, Buccaneers and the Black Flag in the Nineteenth Century*. Cambridge: Cambridge University Press, 2006.

Seymour, Gerald. *The Untouchable*. London: Hodder and Stoughton, 2014.

Sharpe, Christina. *In the Wake: On Blackness and Being*. Durham, NC: Duke University Press, 2016.

Shaviro, Steven. *The Universe of Things: On Speculative Realism*. Minneapolis: University of Minnesota Press, 2014.

Shaikh, Fariha. "*The Alfred* and *The Open Sea*: Periodical Culture and Nineteenth-Century Settler Emigration at Sea." *English Studies in Africa* 57, no. 1 (2014): 21–32.

Shell, R. "Introduction to S. E. Hudson's Slaves." *Kronos* 9 (1984): 44–70.

Sibeko, Oupa. "Bottled Seawater: A Sea Inland." Master's thesis, University of the Witwatersrand, 2020.

Smith, Margaret. *Title-Page: Its Early Development, 1460–1510*. London: British Library, 2001.

South African Railways and Harbours. *Official Railway Tariff Handbook*. Johannesburg: Office of the General Manager of Railways, 1911.

Starosielski, Nicole. "The Elements of Media Studies." *Media+Environment* 1, no. 1 (2019): 1–6.

Stevens, Robert White. *On the Stowage of Ships and Their Cargoes*. Plymouth: Longmans, 1858.

Stewart, Garrett. *Bookwork: Medium to Object to Concept to Art*. Chicago: University of Chicago Press, 2011.

Swyngedouw, Erik. *Liquid Power: Contested Hydro-Modernities in Twentieth-Century Spain*. Cambridge, MA: MIT Press, 2015.

The Tariff Dictionary: A Compendious Handbook to the Fiscal Question. London: Simpkin, Marshall, Hamilton, Kent, n.d.

Taylor, Jesse Oak. *The Sky of Our Manufacture: The London Fog in British Fiction from Dickens to Woolf*. Charlottesville: University of Virginia Press, 2016.

Theal, George McCall, comp. *Records of the Cape Colony*. Vol. 27. London: n.p.

Tide-Waiting, a Poem: Humbly Inscribed to the Hon. Joseph Lysaght, Esq; Collector of the Port of Cork: by the Author, a Tide-Waiter, at Cove. Cork: n.p., 1775.

The Timber Trades Journal List of Shipping Marks. London: Rider, 1920. https://archive.org/details/timbertradesjourshippingmarks/page/n3/mode/2up.

Titlestad, Michael. *Shipwreck Narratives: Out of Our Depth*. London: Palgrave, forthcoming.

Tompkins, Kyla Wazana. "On the Limits and Promise of New Materialist Philosophy." *Lateral* 5, no. 1 (2016). https://doi.org/10.25158/L5.1.8.

Union of South Africa. *Customs Tariff of the Union of South Africa*. Pretoria: Government Printer, 1932.

Union of South Africa. *Customs Tariff of the Union of South Africa*. Pretoria: Government Printer, 1936.

Vahed, Goolam H. "Constructions of Community and Identity among Indians in Colonial Natal, 1860–1910: The Role of the Muharram Festival." *Journal of African History* 43, no. 1 (2002): 77–93.

Vahed, Goolam H. "Mosques, Mawlanas and Muharram: Indian Islam in Colonial Natal, 1860–1910." *Journal of Religion in Africa* 31, no. 3 (2001): 305–35.

Vail, Leroy, and Landeg White. *Power and the Praise Poem: Southern African Voices in History*. Charlottesville: University of Virginia Press, 1991.

Vandenabeele, Louis, Inge Bertels, and Ine Wouters. "Baltic Shipping Marks on Nineteenth-Century Timber: Their Deciphering and a Proposal for Classifying Old Timber." *Construction History* 31, no. 2 (2016): 157–76.

Van der Poel, Jean. *Railway and Customs Policies in South Africa, 1885–1910*. London: Longman Green, 1933.

Vats, Anjali, and Deidré A. Keller. "Critical Race IP." *Cardozo Arts and Entertainment* 36, no. 3 (2018): 735–95.

Viswanathan, Gauri. *Masks of Conquest: Literary Study and British Rule in India*. New York: Columbia University Press, 2014.

Wakefield, Roberta P. *Foreign Marks of Origin Regulations*. Washington: US Department of Commerce, Bureau of Foreign and Domestic Commerce, n.d.

Walcott, Derek. "The Sea Is History." *Collected Poems 1948–1984*. London: Faber and Faber, 1986.

Waugh, Evelyn. *Vile Bodies*. 1930. London: Penguin, 2000.

White, Tim. "The Lovedale Press during the Directorship of R. H. W. Shepherd, 1930–1955." *English in Africa* 19, no. 2 (1992): 69–84.

Wilson, Timothy. *Flags at Sea*. London: Her Majesty's Stationery Office, 1986.

The Wine and Spirit Merchant's Assistant. London: n.p., 1822.

Winkiel, Laura, ed. "Hydrocriticism." Special issue, *English Language Notes* 57, no. 1 (2019): 1–159.

Woodmansee, Martha. "The Genius and the Copyright: Economic and Legal Conditions of the Emergence of the 'Author.'" *Eighteenth-Century Studies* 17, no. 4 (1984): 425–48.

Zalik, Anna. "The Deep Seabed and Colonial Redress." Paper presented at Pedagogies of the Sea, York University, November 20, 2019.

Index

Act of Union, 50
Adelaide, 32
Africa, southern: aquatic territorialism in, 21; Black writers/literature of, 12, 58–61, 78, 81; creolized waters of, 23; Custom House in, 3, 9
Alaimo, Stacy, 18
Algeria, 16
algorithm, 14
Anglo-Boer War (South African War), 66–68
anonymity, 79
apartheid, 14, 73–75, 79
aquafuturist, 23
aquatic territorialism, 21
Ashworth, William, 28
Australia, 32, 51, 63
authorship, 78–80

Barber, Karin, 78–79
Barry, D. G., 67
Behar, Katherine, 8
Belgium, 89n88
Bennett, Jane, 8
Bennett, Joshua, 18
Bently, Lionel, 50
Black hydropoetics, 23
Blue (or Salt) Water principle, 89n88
bodies, 8–9
Bogost, Ian, 7
Book Parts, 77
books: book-as-form, 12; booksellers and, 53–54; cheap US reprints of, 51–52; copyright and, 49–51; copyright stamping the book as white, 3, 57–58; Custom House defines, 11–12; disaggregated into their component parts, 77–78; dockside reading and, 9–13, 78; increase in books entering South Africa, 68–69; landing of, 9–10, 20; as paper commodity, 10; read whole, as objects rather than texts, 3, 10, 15, 65, 68, 83–84; ships' passengers preparing their books for Customs, 49–50; from South Africa, 11; what the colonial book should be and, 11–12. *See also* Custom House; handbook; literature; reading
Borcherds, M., 67
Borges, Jorge Luis, 6
Breckenridge, Keith, 83
British Empire: copyright legislation in, 50–53, 55; Custom House as an institution in, 3, 28–29; mark of origin and, 3, 46–47; South Africa leaving the, 59–60. *See also* colonialism
bureaucracy, 52, 70

Canada, 11, 51
Cape Colony, 39, 66. *See also* South Africa
cargo. *See* objects
Caribbean, the, 17–19
Carroll, Siobhan, 21
censorship: anticommunism in South Africa and, 68–72; apartheid in South Africa and, 14, 73–75; belief that censors are ignorant, 64–65; in context of colonial port, 2–3;

censorship (*continued*)
literature and, 14, 65; military censorship, 74–75; post Anglo-Boer War/South African War, 66–68; sophistication of, 65, 73; time-consuming labor of, 70–71. *See also* Custom House; South Africa
Césaire, Aimé, 18, 88n72
Chan, Suzanna, 23
"Chinese Encyclopedia" (Borges), 6
Chops of the Channel, 49
classifications, 6, 41–42
Cloete, Stuart, 64
coast. *See* littoral
Coetzee, J. M., 12, 74, 82
Cohen, Margaret, 18
Collen, Lindsey, 17
colonialism: anticolonial writers, 79; authority of the nation-state and, 89n88; binaries and, 40; colonial adventure novels and, 81; colonial narrative modes, 12; colonial newspaper, 78–79; colonial object formation and, 8; colonial print culture and, 3; colonized water and, 21–22; as a copyright on civilization, 60; erasure of the ocean via, 19; submarine engineering and, 36–37; what the colonial book should be, 11–12. *See also* British Empire; hydrocolonialism; postcolonialism
Colony of Natal (Ingram), 81
Committee against the Ban on Working Class Literature, 68
communism, 68–72
Congo, 89n88
Conrad, Joseph, 4
coolies, 30
copyright: African writers and, 58–61; alternative histories of, 61–62; booksellers and merchants using copyright to outwit competitors, 53–54, 59; colonialism as a copyright on civilization, 60; confusion around, 50–55, 62; contemporary debates on, 61; in context of colonial port, 2–3; epidemiological viewing of, 59–60; infringements of, 53–54; legislation in the British Empire, 50–53, 55; mark of origin and, 46, 57; as a sign of propriety, 3, 20, 52–53, 58, 62; as white, 3, 57–58, 60. *See also* Custom House; mark of origin; Merchandise Marks Act of 1887; race
Copyright Amendment Act of 1842, 51
counterindication, 47
COVID-19, 84
Crain, Patricia, 13
creolized water, 22–24
Criminal Law of False Marking. *See* Merchandise Marks Act of 1887
Custom House: as an institution in British Empire, 3, 28–29; carceral language/traditions of, 9, 36, 64, 68; classifications and, 6; conflicting ideas about what constituted authority and initiative at, 53; customs manuals and, 10–11; defines the book, 11–12; extends its influence into the ocean, 30–32; flags and, 32–33; frontage of, 33; immigration restriction via, 9, 35–36, 64, 68; location of the, 23, 30; naval modes of authority influence the, 32–34; ships' passengers preparing their books for, 49–50; slavery and, 8–9, 29–30; in southern Africa, 3, 9. *See also* books; censorship; copyright; customs officials; objects; reading
customs manuals, 10–11
customs officials: admiration for the navy, 24, 33–34; classifying objects, 6; confusion around copyright and, 50, 55–56; intimate knowledge of objects, 45, 47–48; involvement with slavery, 29–30; literary representations of, 13; patterns of residence of, 34; treatment of books, 10. *See also* Custom House

da Cunha, Dilip, 16
De dochter van den handsopper (The daughter of the hands-upper) (Reitz), 66–67
DeLoughrey, Elizabeth, 21
Department of the Interior, 72
detention on information, 53
"Die Stem van Suid-Afrika," 59
disease, 4, 8–9
"Docks, Cape Town" (Barry and Borcherds), 67
dockside reading: bodies and, 8–9; books and, 9–13, 78; definition of, 4; genres of the dockside and, 11–13; interaction between officials, object, and environment in, 41;

objects and, 4–8; reading methods of, 13–15, 43–44, 65. *See also* hydrocolonialism; reading
dockworkers, 23, 42–43
dredging, 22, 37
Drexciya, 23
dry technologies, 22
Durban. *See* South Africa
Dutch rule, 9, 23–24

ecopoetics, 17–18
elemental media studies, 20
Ellis Island, 9
English Channel, 49
Escombe, Harry, 35–36
Excise, 28

"Farm Novel and *Plaasroman*" (Coetzee), 82
farm novel: link to shipwreck narrative, 12–13, 82–83
film, 71–72
flags, 32–33
folktales, 79
Foreign Reprints Act, 51–52
Foucault, Michel, 6

Gallagher, Ellen, 23
Gandhi, Mohandas, 36, 79–80
genre, 11–12
Germany, 58
Ghosh, Amitav, 17
Gitelman, Lisa, 10
Glover, Kaiama, 18
Gordimer, Nadine, 14, 64–65
Government Gazette, 52
Great Expectations (Dickens), 19

Haiti, 17–18
Hall, John, 63
Hammett, Ivo, 64–65
handbook: customs manuals and, 10–11; as a genre of the dockside, 12; to record shipping marks, 44; settler handbook, 80; tariff handbook and, 6–7. *See also* books; literature
harbor engineer, 22
Harman, Graham, 7–8

Harney, Stefano, 9
Hawthorne, Nathaniel, 13
Heath, Deana, 64
Hindu creation myths, 37
Hindu-Muslim festivals, 23
hurricane, 17–18
hydrocolonial irrigation, 16
hydrocolonialism: bringing naval modes of authority onto land as, 32–34; colonized water and, 21–22; definition of, 15–16; extending authority over the ocean as, 30–32; forms of authorship, 80; hydrocolonial print cultures and, 20; as a turn towards multidirectional empire-wide interactions, 19. *See also* colonialism; dockside reading
hydrocolonic, 16
hydrocolony, 16
hydrocracy, 24
hydrocriticism, 21, 88n52
hydroimaginaries, 17, 24
hydroimperialism, 16
hydrology, 19

Illustrated London News, 39–40, 42
immigrants, 8, 12
immigration restriction, 8, 35, 58, 68
In an Antique Land: History in the Guise of a Traveler's Tale (Ghosh), 17
indentured laborers, 29–30
India, 52
Indian Ocean, 17, 19
Indian Opinion, 79
Indigenous, 82
Ingram, J. Forsyth, 80, 83
Innes, Edward, 37
Ireland, 50
Ivan Tavlov, 71

Jamaica, 30
Jeffries, James, 57
jinn, 23, 37, 90n98
Joffee, Louis, 69
Johns, Adrian, 62
Johnson, Jack, 57
Justice Department, 55

Lagos, 22
landing, 5, 9–10, 20, 36–37, 39–43; authorship as, 80
landing waiter, 39–41
Lavery, Charne, 19
Lawrence and Wishart, 70
Lighton, R. E., 74
lists, 7
literature: anticolonial and antiapartheid writers, 79; atmospheric methods and, 17, 21; censorship and, 65; elemental methods and, 17, 19–20; farm novel and, 12, 82–83; hydrological cycle and, 16–17; land reclamation and, 12, 21, 87n40; littoral literature and, 18, 81; megascale meteorological patterns in, 17–18; modern digital literary criticism, 14; oceanography and, 18; port infrastructure and, 12, 20–21, 78, 80; postcolonial literary criticism, 17–18; representations of customs officials in, 13; southern African literature and, 12, 68–71, 78, 81; story of the shipwreck and, 12, 80–81. *See also* books; handbook; spiralism
littoral: as amphibious, 18; as coastal form, 18; communication on, 5; as ecotone, 18; instrumentalization of, 37; shipwrecks and, 81
Long Room, 34–35

mark of origin, 3, 46–47, 57–58. *See also* copyright
marks and numbers, 43–44
masulah boats, 24
Mathur, Anuradha, 16
McCormack, Derek, 20
McDonald, Peter, 73
McGill, Meredith, 13, 58–59
Mendelsohn, Ben, 22, 82
Merchandise Marks Act of 1887, 46, 53, 55–56. *See also* copyright
Merchandise Marks Manual, 53
Middle Passage, 23
Miller, Thomas Maskew, 54–55
monsoons, 17
Moscow Daily News, 69
Moten, Fred, 9
Mutiny (Collen), 17

Navigation Acts, 28–29
Netherlands, 73
Newell, Stephanie, 78–79
newspaper, 78–79
Nuttall, Sarah, 18

objects: books read as, 3, 10, 15, 65, 68, 83–84; colonial object formation and, 8; customs officials' intimate knowledge of, 45, 47–48; dockside reading and, 4–8; influence on dockside protocols, 6; landing of, 41–43; object ontologies, 7–8, 42, 48; techniques used for identifying cargo transferred to people, 8–9; that fall under suspicion, 5, 43–45. *See also* Custom House
ocean, 19, 24, 30–32, 37
oceanic studies: critical oceanic studies, 17, 22; oceanic turn, 81; oceanography and literature, 18; vertical ocean, 19
Old Drift, The (Serpell), 19
oral forms, 79
oral poetry, 79

Patents, Designs, Trade Marks and Copyright Act of 1916, 52
People's Bookshop, 70
Peters, John Durham, 20
Philip, M. NourbeSe, 18
plantation, 28–29
poetry, 79
port cities: colonization of water around, 21–22; immigration-restriction policies and, 8; objects in, 4–8; regulatory media and regimes of identification in, 4; slavery and, 9; from a submarine perspective, 22
Port Elizabeth, 39
postcolonialism, 15–19. *See also* colonialism
Pritchard, Sara, 16, 19
propriety, 3, 20, 52–53, 58, 62
pseudonymity, 79
Publication Control Board, 74

race, 3, 8, 37, 57–58, 60–61. *See also* copyright; whiteness
reading: books as objects, rather than texts, 3, 10, 15, 65, 68, 83–84; dockside reading

methods, 13–15, 43–44, 65; epidemiological reading method, 15, 45–46, 72, 83–84; slow reading, 79–80. *See also* books; Custom House; dockside reading
Reitz, Hjalmar, 66–67
Rubusana, W. B., 60–61
Rutherford, George, 27–30, 33–35

Samuelson, Meg, 18
Scarlet Letter, The (Hawthorne), 13
Schreiner, Olive, 82
"Sea Is History, The" (Walcott), 18
Searle, Dick, 63
Secker and Warburg, 74
Serpell, Namwali, 19
Sharpe, Christina, 21
Shaviro, Steven, 7
shipping marks, 43–44
shipwreck, 12, 80–81
shore people, 4
slavery, 9, 23, 29–30, 58
slow reading, 79–80
South Africa: books from, 11; censorship and Anglo-Boer War/South African War of 1899–1902, 65–68; censorship and anticommunism in, 68–72; censorship and apartheid in, 14, 73–75; Customs and Excise Department, 1–2; Durban's port infrastructure and, 37; immigration restriction and, 35; increase in books entering, 68–69; landing in ports in, 5; leaving the British Commonwealth, 59–60; literature of, 12; slavery and, 30. *See also* censorship
South African Society for Peace and Friendship, 71
South African War (Anglo-Boer War), 66–68
speculative realists, 7
spiralism, 17–18. *See also* literature
spiritscapes, 37
Starosielski, Nicole, 20
Stationers' Hall, 62
Story of an African Farm (Schreiner), 82
Story of an African Seaport, The: Being the History of the Port and Borough of Durban, the Seaport of Natal, (Ingram), 80
"Struggle of the Bolsheviks for the Social Insurance of the Proletariat, The," 68
submarine engineering, 21–22, 36–37
Swyngedouw, Erik, 19
Sydney. *See* Australia

tallyers, 43
tariff handbook, 6–7, 41
"Tasters in Chief—the Customs Story," 64
Taylor, Jesse Oak, 21
telegraph, 44
thread count, 44
Titlestad, Michael, 12
Transvaal Surrounded, The, 57
Trevelyan, Charles, 52
Turning Wheels (Cloete), 64

underwater methods: African ancestors and, 23; going below the waterline, 18, 22, 37; harbor floor method, 22–23, 90n96; submarine aesthetics, 22, 90n94; submarine cosmopolitanism, 22, 37
United States, 47, 51

Vechten en vlugten van Beyers en Kemp (Advance and retreat of Beyers and Kemp) (Naude), 67

Waiting for the Barbarians (Coetzee), 74
Walcott, Derek, 18
water: colonized, 21–22; creolized, 22–23; as political authority, 16; as social substance, 16–17
watermeisie, 90n98
water spirits, 23
whiteness, 3, 57–58, 60. *See also* race
Wren, Christopher, 35
writing and dictation test, 58

Zemk'inkomo magwalandini (Rubusana), 60

www.ingramcontent.com/pod-product-compliance
Lightning Source LLC
Chambersburg PA
CBHW050554160426
43199CB00015B/2661